Left, Right, Out:
The History of Third Parties
in America

Printed in the United States of America

First Printing, 2012

ISBN 978-0-578-10654-0

Arts and Letters Imperium Publishing
www.LeftRightOut.com

To my parents, for instilling in me their love of America and her history, and a passion for the written word.

Contents

Introduction

The greatest misconception concerning American politics is that the nation has always been built upon a two-party system. Many would be surprised to learn that the United States was, in fact, founded with the intent that there should be no political parties. Instead, the framers of the Constitution envisioned a nation of political consensus. The earliest political writings of the founding fathers demonstrate a deep antipathy to political factions and the authors of the Constitution felt that the ultimate goal for the new nation must be unity above all else: unity of purpose, unity of principle, and unity of politics. Without such unity, it was feared, the Great Experiment was destined to fail.

Shortly after the nation's founding, fear of factionalism gave way to emerging and divergent interpretations of what America should and would become. Centered upon the politics and personalities of Alexander Hamilton and Thomas Jefferson, two factions soon formed within the body politic. These factions eventually become the first political parties. Though quite different from today's parties, the Federalists and the Anti-Federalists, as the two ideologies were initially known, soon came to dominate the political discourse in the young republic. This early division of American politics into two camps would define – and limit – the nation's politics to the present day.

But the two-party system has not gone unchallenged. Notwithstanding America's enduring bilateral political division, third parties have emerged again and again. These movements, each a response to unique historical conditions in the United States, have all left some legacy in the American political system, the American economy, or American society as a whole. The nature of this legacy, and its extent, depends largely on the nature of the party. In understanding and

6

evaluating each third party and its lasting impact on the United States, it is helpful to consider whether a party can generally be categorized as *Realignment* or *Doctrinal* in nature.

Realignment parties serve to alter the political system and influence the policy-making process of the major parties. On the one hand, Realignment party candidates can pose a threat to one of the major parties, either by being a viable alternative to a major party and its candidate, or by siphoning off votes from a party or candidate more closely associated with the positions of the third party. To counter this threat, major parties frequently appropriate certain policy positions of the third parties challenging them for their traditional constituency. In recent years, the major parties have also sought to cynically manipulate third party ballot access to ensure or prevent third parties from siphoning or splitting votes of like-minded voters.

In the past few election cycles, Democrats have fought to keep the Green Party and its candidates off the ballot in several states, while the Republicans have provided resources in order to assist Green Party Candidates in gaining ballot access. Conversely, in 2010 there were reports of fake candidates carrying the banner of the "Tea Party" movement, who were sponsored and directed by local Democratic Party activists, in order to split the conservative vote. There is perhaps no greater testament to the impact and import of third parties than the lengths taken by the major parties to blunt their effect and manipulate them to their advantage.

The contemporary schism within the Republican Party over the nature of American conservatism has taken on genuine and potentially long-lasting Realignment qualities, with Libertarians and self-proclaimed "Tea-Party Activists" challenging establishment Republicans within the primary or general election process. The outcome of the emergence of the "Tea Party," while not a formal political party in its own right, is yet to be seen. However, victories by "Tea Party" supported candidates against Republican Party favorites in several primaries and their inclusion in a Republican-majority Congress does tend to foretell a realignment within the Republican Party as opposed to the emergence of a separate political party. Should the Tea Party movement ultimately cleave off from the GOP, its nature and impact as a true third party will surely be far different than if it were to remain within the Republican Party; it could transform itself into more of a doctrinal party focused on a limited core set of issues such as a balanced budget and immigration. As will been seen throughout the book, however, Realignment, is rarely, if ever, achieved in a single election cycle.

On the other hand, Realignment Parties have, occasionally, been the source of innovation in the political process itself and not the internal workings and direction of a particular major party. In those cases the change was immediately visible. It was the Anti-Masons who first organized a national nominating convention and adopted a party platform. The major parties of the time quickly emulated the Anti-Masonic Party and have continued ever since. What were novelties in the early 1830s have today become a staple of the Republican and Democratic parties, as well as all other political parties seeking viability during presidential election years.

Other third parties, best described as Doctrinal in nature, are less concerned with electoral success than with adherence to vision and principle. This lack of focus on winning elections does not necessarily lessen the impact of doctrinal parties. Unquestionably, one of the most successful third parties in American history was the doctrinal Prohibition Party. Founded in 1869 to fight against the manufacture, sale and consumption of alcoholic beverages in the United States, the Prohibition Party is the oldest surviving third party in the United States. The ratification of the 18th Amendment represents the culmination of decades of effort by the party. Though a short-lived victory (the 21st Amendment, which became law in 1933, reversed the prohibition imposed by the 18th amendment, which had been ratified a mere 14 years earlier), no other Doctrinal party can point to any achievement with as far-reaching significance as the Prohibition Party. Further, while Prohibition itself was short-lived, the impact on society of this failed experiment continues to be felt today.

As the Republican - Tea Party - Libertarian struggle mentioned above plays out, those conservatives and libertarians who opt to campaign independently of the Republican Party may ultimately be more accurately described as Doctrinal rather than Realignment. Much will depend on how the Republican Party chooses to govern and how long the self-described "Tea Party" candidates remain in elected office. Likewise, while hoping to affect wholesale changes in American politics and society, the Green Party essentially espouses doctrinal politics, namely, environmentalism. Both these movements, the "Tea Party" and political environmentalism, are clearly in their infancy. American third party history can be a guide in understanding their viability and predicting their future impact.

What is so fascinating about the study of America's forgotten third party history is the great dynamism it exposes in our society and political culture. In just the last twenty years, three movements – the Reform Party, the Green Party, and the "Tea Party" – have all profoundly affected the outcomes of elections at the national level. In at least two cases the evidence suggests that third parties ultimately decided the presidency. Given the clear examples of third party influence and importance today, it is vital to understand this history to better understand our present and future.

Each third party in American history, whether Realignment, Doctrinal, or possessing hybrid characteristics of the two, has been conspicuously unsuccessful in national campaigns – with a lone exception. The Republican Party possesses the unique distinction amongst third parties as having made the transition from a nascent alliance of disparate interests to major party status. Though often assumed to be a permanent fixture in the duopoly of political power in the United States, the Republican Party was a late-comer to the game, having only been formed in the middle of the nineteenth century. Therefore it is with no small amount of irony that the party is often referred to as the Grand Old Party. Since the ossification of the current two-party system, American presidents have been overwhelmingly Democrat or Republican. Indeed, with the exception of a mere two Whigs,[1] every elected president since Andrew Jackson has hailed from either side of this political divide.

The general lack of electoral success notwithstanding, third parties and their candidates have made impressive showings in several elections at all levels of government. The Socialist Party, whose support peaked at 6 percent of the popular vote in the presidential election of 1912, repeatedly managed to elect mayors in several large cities including Milwaukee, Wisconsin and Bridgeport, Connecticut. Populist governors ran Kansas, Colorado and North Dakota during the 1890s. For nearly a century after 1850, the United States Congress regularly included a small number of representatives from various third parties: Free Soil in the 1850s, Greenback in the 1870s, Populist in the 1890s, and even Socialist in the 1910s, to name a few.

In the 1848 election, former Democratic President and then-Free Soil Party candidate Martin Van Buren won 10 percent of the popular vote. With the demise of what historians call the Second Party System in the 1850s, the American Party (also called the "Know-Nothing" Party as a political epithet by its opponents), Constitutional, and Republican parties emerged as a result of the disarray and

---

[1] Two other Whigs, John Tyler and Millard Fillmore, ascended to the presidency when the incumbent Whig presidents with whom they served as vice-president, William Henry Harrison and James Tyler, respectively, died in office.

10

disintegration of the then-major parties, the Whigs and the Democrats. Since the Civil War, five third party candidates have captured votes in the electoral college: General James B. Weaver, Populist Party candidate in 1892; Theodore Roosevelt, Progressive (Bull Moose) Party candidate in 1912; Robert LaFollette, Progressive Party candidate in 1924, Strom Thurmond, States' Rights (Dixiecrat) Party candidate in 1948; and George Wallace, American Independent Party candidate in 1968. In that same span, seven third party candidates have garnered more than 5 percent of the popular vote: Weaver; Roosevelt; LaFollette; Wallace; Eugene Debs, the Socialist Party candidate in 1912; John Anderson, Independent Party candidate in 1980; and Ross Perot as both independent and Reform Party candidate in 1992 and 1996, respectively. In 1912, Roosevelt outpolled the then-sitting president, William Taft, splitting the Republican vote and putting a grateful Woodrow Wilson in the Oval Office. Win or lose (and clearly the outcome is most often lose), third party candidates affect election outcomes.

While the third party track record is not completely devoid of success, third parties have, for the most part, been relegated to the dustbin of political history as fringe movements. This brings us to an important question: given the inability of third parties to conquer the presidency or create a concrete, uniform legacy, how are they relevant to American history, let alone America's future? An American thinking "third party" today will, at best, conjure a mental image of an eccentric, jug-eared billionaire from Texas or a dour consumer rights activist-*cum*-politician. Surely this association does not augur well for the future of an alternate choice in American politics. With Democrats and Republicans sustaining what can only be described as an adversarial duopoly on power, what need is there for an examination of third party politics in America?

The reality is that third parties are akin to the great rivers that have forged the American landscape. Third parties have reshaped America's political

11

landscape; a constant reality capable of altering the political landscape incrementally but irrevocably. Examined side-by-side and in their proper historical context, third parties serve to expose the most acute social, political and economic forces affecting American culture and politics, and they reveal an important yet oft-overlooked response to these phenomena. By studying the conditions in which a given third party develops and those championing its cause, we can attain a degree of understanding unavailable through the typical and often perfunctory stride through the annals of American history. The key, then, is to view third parties as the expository mirrors of change in American political history. Such a study both facilitates and augments an understanding of the prevailing forces that came to define America as it exists today. And, as noted, this historical understanding prepares us to recognize and comprehend the same forces as they play out in the present and beyond.

Beyond the contextual and temporal relevance of third parties, part of understanding their importance is appreciating the tremendous difficulty associated with the third party vote. From the nation's founding, the chips have been stacked heavily against third parties and their candidates. Three major barriers prevent outside parties from having a steady, perceptible impact on American politics: constitutional constraints; legislative restrictions; and limited resources.

First, constraints inherent in the constitutional scheme weigh heavily against an outside party's ascension. Structural limitations, ancillary to the constitutional design, militate heavily towards perpetuating a winner-takes-all system. Parties or individuals obtaining a mere plurality win; the narrowness of their margin of victory is moot; even obtaining a majority is irrelevant.

Secondly, direct legislative limitations, most often in the form of state ballot access restrictions, serve to tightly limit the options available to voters on Election Day. A third party running a national campaign must not only work

12

within constitutional and federal legal boundaries, but must also abide by each state's unique and often divergent ballot access laws. In other words, to merely ensure that its candidate is eligible to receive *a single vote*, a third party must be sophisticated enough to navigate this legal maze without losing sight of its national agenda.

Finally, it has grown exceedingly difficult for a third party to raise the immense financial resources readily available to the established parties. In the 2004 presidential campaigns, spending by candidates leapt more than 50% from levels reached just four years earlier to top $1 billion dollars for the first time in history. Candidates' parties and independent groups together spent nearly $4 billion. The amount spent by and on behalf of President Barack Obama and his opponent, Senator John McCain, reached a staggering $5.3 billion in the 2008 campaign. Today, in the wake of the *Citizens United v. Federal Election Commission*[2] Supreme Court ruling, it seems only more likely that these numbers will continue their stratospheric trajectory.

Having near-limitless resources, the ability to drum up tremendous funds on short notice, national recognition and no shortage of press coverage, the major parties are ensconced in the national psyche as the only available options. H. Ross Perot's relative success in gaining media attention during his 1992 and 1996 campaigns owed no small part to his personal financial resources and his eccentric personality. However, few third parties or their candidates are in a position to compete with the major parties in spending, recognition, or coverage.

The personal or political notoriety of a third party candidate could elevate the visibility and credibility of a third party. Such recognition lessens the impact of and need for substantial financial assets to begin or sustain a campaign. Former presidents Martin Van Buren and Theodore Roosevelt ran strong campaigns as

---

[2] 558 U.S. 50; 130 S.Ct. 876 (2010)

13

third party candidates after their presidencies. Presently, however, a third-party presidential campaign by a former president seems unlikely and risks appearing rather pathetic to the public.[3] Such a candidacy though, would help to dampen the financial imbalance serving to perpetuate the two-party system. No former president, though, has run as a third-party candidate in the modern political and media age to test the theory.

In the past, political parties were more a coalition of local and state chapters with less national party allegiance. Improved transportation and communications shifted the major parties from a coalition of local and state chapters, into centralized national organizations. The media followed suit and the role of presidents and presidential candidates rose enormously relative to local politicians in dictating the fortunes of the party at the ballot box.

Throughout the 19th century, third parties, while largely unsuccessful campaigning for the presidency, could console themselves in the knowledge that they would exert influence from the various city, state, and national elections they would win. However, like the major parties, for much of the twentieth century each third party has been represented almost exclusively by their presidential

---

[3] Since Van Buren and Roosevelt ran as third party candidates, the 22nd Amendment was ratified. The 22nd Amendment prohibits individuals from serving more than two terms as president. Therefore, only one-term presidents may run again. The two living former presidents that would not be constitutionally barred from running for office are Jimmy Carter and George H.W. Bush. It is difficult to imagine a scenario in which either of these men would run for president again, least of all as a third party candidate. For one, George H.W. Bush is no extremist, and conceiving of him either finding a more ideologically well-suited party for him than the GOP, or that he would be so partisan as to gravitate toward third-party politics, is beyond my powers of imagination. Jimmy Carter, on the other hand, is more ideologically driven in his politics. The problem is that the left in America has a paucity of parties from which to choose. The only obvious alternative to the Democratic Party for Carter, the Green Party, no doubt espouses positions with which Carter agrees, but not about which he is passionate. Carter has elected to pursue humanitarian work in his post-presidency, not the environment. Despite Carter's friendship with Communist Cuban Dictator Fidel Castro, Carter does not appear to be a Communist or harbor extreme Socialist leanings; either way, all former presidents care too much about their legacies to run for any of the myriad Socialist- and Communist-affiliated parties in the United States. Finally, recall that most living voters expressed their desire that neither of these men serve as President again the last time they were given the chance.

14

nominee. With presidential electoral success elusive, third parties risk being permanently left out of the political system in its current state. Perhaps a coalition of current and former elected officials is needed in the modern age. A group of high profile candidates would draw attention to the party as a whole, not just its presidential candidate. Having several political figures running simultaneously, at all levels of government, would also provide a greater possibility of some candidates overcoming the electoral obstacles placed in the path of third parties.

As many know, the American voting system – a "first-past-the-post" system – elects legislators based on geographical district by majority or plurality. In such a system, a party gaining a one-vote plurality in every election district wins 100 percent of the seats in the legislature. This outcome stands in marked contrast to those of the parliamentary systems more commonly found abroad. In a parliamentary system, legislators are typically elected "at-large" – that is, voters vote for a party rather than a specific candidate. After the election, the total number of votes a party receives determines the number of legislative seats the party is granted. Individual legislators are chosen from a list made public before the election and only the smallest of parties are kept out of legislative bodies by minimum thresholds their parties must surmount.[4]

The first-past-the-post system greatly favors a two-party system. The parliamentary system makes multi-party governments substantially more likely, as any one party garnering enough votes for a single seat in Parliament can make its voice heard nationally. Having a national spokesperson is one of the greatest assets a minor party can muster, which is why personalities such as Perot and Jessie "the Body" Ventura did much to make the Reform Party a legitimate threat to the Democratic and Republican duopoly during the 1990s. The recognition of this

---

[4] Such election thresholds range dramatically from country to country in attempting to strike a balance between representation, governability, and government stability. In countries such as Portugal and South Africa the threshold is set at zero, whereas in Turkey the figure is as high as 10 percent.

phenomenon is most acutely apparent in the reaction to Perot's appearance in the 1992 presidential campaign.

Following Perot's idiosyncratic performance in the 1992 presidential debates between himself, the incumbent president George H. W. Bush, and then-Governor of Arkansas Bill Clinton, Perot's support more than doubled. Perot's surge in popular support went beyond the mere capture of votes cast, but actually put him within striking distance of securing votes in the Electoral College.[5] Never again have the major parties allowed a third party candidate to participate in presidential debates. The risk of validating or drawing attention to the personality of the candidate, and thus the third party, is too great. It is also the one thing that money and system restraints cannot control. Success by Perot, or any modern third party presidential candidate, in capturing even a single Electoral College vote would have the potential to change the minds of voters, and thus American politics, forever. For this reason, so much is done by the major parties to ensure it does not happen.

There is no more notorious American political institution than the oft-despised and commonly misunderstood Electoral College. In conjunction with the first-past-the-post system, the Electoral College system is strongly biased against national third parties. Failure to earn popular vote pluralities in any state, no matter the vote count, ensures failure in the Electoral College. Moreover, the Electoral College system can often lead to strange results despite what would seem otherwise obvious based on the popular vote. For example, in 1980 John Anderson, the National Unity Party candidate, won nearly 7% of the popular vote, but failed to win a single electoral vote. On the other hand, in 1948, Strom Thurmond, as the States' Rights Party candidate, won 39 electoral votes (roughly 8% of the total)

---

[5] Perot suffered from a paradox of third party presidential campaigning. In securing nation-wide support he failed to dominate in any individual state or region. He finished second in Maine and Utah, and captured several counties spread across seven states throughout the country.

16

with only 2.5% of the popular vote. But whatever the outcome in popular or electoral votes, interest in and support of third party candidates remains a mainstay of U.S. politics and the electorate.

Today, interest in a viable third party comes from major media as well as the general public. Conjecture abounds that independent and independent-minded politicians could launch a centrist party, allowing the Democratic and Republican parties to continue their current polarizing trajectories. New York Mayor Michael Bloomberg, former Governor Charlie Christ of Florida, as well as former Senators Chuck Hegel and Evan Bayh, usually top the list of those politicians with enough name recognition and centrist credentials to help launch such a movement. The geographic diversity of the names on this list (major cities and states, along with the Great Lakes and Midwest) alone helps to make even the notion of such a development a potent threat to the present duopoly. Add together the personal financial resources and fund-raising capabilities of the above-named prospective candidates, and a potential and potent third party becomes quite imaginable. In fact, such a change would prove not merely one of Realignment, but likely revolutionary.

All this information still begs the question: why *this* book on third parties? Currently, the limited writings on third parties fail to explore the subject in a sufficiently thorough manner. One problem lies in the method employed by scholars to approach the examination of third parties. Often, an author will devote his or her attention to one party or movement at a time. Thus, there is no shortage of literature on the rise of the Bull Moose Party, the Prohibitionists, or the Socialists, as these parties are among the most well known. This piecemeal examination of distinct third parties is useful as reference – however, for readers in search of an expansive review of third parties throughout American history,

17

identifying which works will, collectively, present a comprehensive history of third parties can be daunting if not impossible.

Alternatively, various writers have sought to discuss third parties indirectly through an examination of the American political system. In such cases, third parties become anecdotes or even footnotes in a broader, more standardized chronicling of American political history. The prime example is the election of 1912, in which the Socialist and Bull Moose Parties played significant roles, albeit in the eventual election of Democrat Woodrow Wilson. Nonetheless they receive little mention in contemporary or historical reviews of their impact.

This book takes a different approach. Rather than merely explore the rise and fall of a single third party, or gloss over the very existence of one or more third parties, *Left, Right, Out* examines each significant third party throughout American history. By studying third parties in the order in which they arrived on the political scene, the author seeks to impart a degree of contextual support absent in previous works in order to shed light on third party philosophy, evolution, and impact from one generation to the next. By considering third parties chronologically, this book develops an approach – steeped in political history and thought – in charting the history and predicting the future of third party politics in America. While the exact future of third parties in the United States is uncertain to be sure, such a vibrant history and tangible present assuredly portends great reason for optimism for third party prospects looking ahead.

The Birth of a Nation,

The Birth of Parties:

The Federalists and Anti-Federalists

[Parties] are likely, in the course of time and things, to become potent engines, by which cunning, ambitious, and unprincipled men will be enabled to subvert the power of the people, and to usurp for themselves the reins of government.

– George Washington's
"Farewell Address", 1796

It is surprising to some that national politics predated the birth of the American nation. Yet the very process by which the United States was formed, the Constitutional Convention, pitted the "Federalists," led by Alexander Hamilton, against the "Anti-Federalists," led by Thomas Jefferson. These factions engaged in a struggle to define the character of the new nation and the balance of powers between state and national governments. The Federalists, as their name implies, sought to strengthen the federal government to remedy what were viewed as the great shortcomings of the then-operating Articles of Confederation. The Anti-Federalists, on the other hand, sought to direct the convention (and the Constitution) toward a weaker federal government and greater deference to state sovereignty and emphasis on individual civil liberties.

Despite the factionalism during the convention, the development of a two-party system was nearly impossible to foresee. Philosophical disputes aside, the nation's founders abhorred party politics: George Washington called for "vigilance to prevent" parties, while Jefferson remarked that, were it impossible to "go to heaven but with a party," he would rather "not go there at all." Hamilton, and Anti-Federalist James Madison, authors of *The Federalist Papers*, warned of the "avarice" and "mischief" of parties. Fears that factionalism would prevail seemed unfounded when, as the Constitution was adopted and the Anti-Federalist's fears were assuaged by the ratification of the Bill of Rights, it appeared the nation was settling into a non-partisan status quo.

In the nation's first gathering of the Electoral College, George Washington was elected unanimously by all 69 electors. The strongest voice of the Anti-Federalist movement, Thomas Jefferson, had been brought into the administration as Secretary of State and formed part of Washington's first cabinet alongside Alexander Hamilton. In the first Congress, three-quarters of the House of Representatives and over half the members of the Senate identified with the

20

Federalists who had achieved the drafting and ratification of the new constitution. However, this harmony was not to last. Despite the compromises reached during the Constitutional Convention and the protections provided by the Bill of Rights, the Federalists began to impose their vision for the nation in the interpretation and application of the powers granted by the new constitution to the national government. These policies, along with acute personal differences, eventually pushed the Anti-Federalists from this seeming unity government.

Due to their long history of shared military service and a strong personal relationship, Hamilton enjoyed substantial influence within Washington's administration. As Treasury Secretary, Hamilton called for ambitious national economic programs, including a national bank and the assumption of state debt by the national government. Initially supportive of some of Hamilton's programs (Jefferson helped steer the assumption of state debt through Congress in exchange for locating the nation's capitol on the banks of the Potomac River), the Secretary of State began to question the wisdom of the government's policies.

In 1791 Jefferson set out with fellow Virginian James Madison on a trip through the Northeast. During this trip Jefferson and Madison are believed to have met with Robert Livingston and George Clinton, powerful New York political figures and rivals of Alexander Hamilton; they are also believed to have met with Aaron Burr. Burr was in the process of establishing a political society known as Tammany that would dominate New York City politics from the colonial era up until the New Deal. Burr, no friend of Hamilton politically, would famously (and fatally) wound him in a duel on the banks of the Hudson River in Weehawken, New Jersey. These meetings between the New York and Virginia leaders formed the basis for a political alliance between wealthy southern landowners and the northern merchant class that was to craft national policy for nearly 150 years.

A more politically diverse Second Congress resulted in more firmly defined and divisive factions. On any given matter before the House of Representatives, over 40% of the members voted consistently with Madison, the *de facto* opposition leader to Hamilton's agenda, and control of the Senate actually shifted from members identified as pro-administration, and thus Federalist, to those generally considered anti-administration and Anti-Federalist. Consensus turned to friction – at times rising to vitriol.

Keeping in the tradition that brought forth the intellectual and impassioned writing of the Declaration of Independence, the Constitution and the Federalist Papers, these emerging factions brandished the weapon of the day: the pen. The *Gazette of the United States*, a Philadelphia newspaper run by John Fenno, became a mouthpiece for Hamilton's agenda and was funded with generous advertising dollars from the Treasury Department. Madison and Jefferson struck back, helping to establish the *National Gazette* by putting Philip Freneau, the paper's publisher and Yale classmate of Jefferson, on the State Department's payroll as a clerk. With such clear lines drawn within government and the press, the parties, though not formal, nor named, had arrived.

In a letter written shortly before his death, Jefferson described his view of the political world. In it, Jefferson expresses his belief that dichotomous politics is the natural state of things. To Jefferson, individuals

> by their constitutions are naturally divided into two parties: 1. Those who fear and distrust the people, and wish to draw all powers from them into the hands of the higher classes. 2. Those who identify themselves with the people, have confidence in them, cherish and consider them as the most honest and safe, although not the most wise depositary of the public interests. In every country these two parties exist, and in every one where they are free to think, speak, and write, they will declare themselves. Call them, therefore, liberals and serviles, Jacobins and Ultras, whigs and tories, republicans and federalists, aristocrats and democrats, or by whatever name you please, they are the same parties still and pursue

the same object. The last appellation of aristocrats and democrats is the true one expressing the essence of all.

While not addressing the notion of formal political parties, this view would be played out in the elections of 1796 and 1800. Despite his expressed abhorrence of political parties, it seems Jefferson believed them to be, at least in hindsight, inevitable.

During the second presidential election, in 1792, the Anti-Federalists were far better organized and the Congressional opposition emerged onto the national political scene. Though Washington again secured a unanimous vote of the 132 electors, John Adams's reelection as Vice-president came with only 77 votes to New York's Anti-Federalist governor George Clinton's 50. While the Father of His Country was immune to the growing political schisms, all other parts of American politics were beginning to divide along the Hamiltonian/Federalist and Jeffersonian/Anti-Federalist lines.

Domestic divisions grew starker as the national debate spilled out into international affairs. The French Revolution was viewed by many Anti-Federalists as an extension of the fight for liberty from which the United States had so recently emerged. With France's declaration of war on Britain in 1793, many advocated that the nation should take up arms in this perceived sister revolution. Washington, however, was swift to declare the nation's neutrality, disappointing Jefferson, a strong supporter of the French cause. Jefferson resigned as Secretary of State that same year.

Eventually France's supporters formed political clubs alternately known as either "Democratic" or "Republic" to note their backing of the anti-monarchial revolution. These clubs took to campaigning on behalf of the Anti-Federalist candidates for Congress who were swiftly becoming known as Republicans or Democratic-Republicans.

With Washington's decision not to stand for a third term in the 1796 election, Republicans implicitly understood they would support Jefferson for president. Federalist members of Congress met to coordinate their efforts and agreed to cast their votes for Adams for president and Thomas Pickney for vice president. When the Electoral College met, however, the vote was split, with Adams securing the presidency and Jefferson the Vice Presidency. Though this divided government may have been ideal for some of the Founders, the response to this outcome, the ratification of the 12th Amendment in 1804, forever changed the Electoral College to ensure that the President and Vice President would come from the same party ticket. The divided Adams-Jefferson administration was wrought with acrimony between the two men. Indeed, the permanent polarization of American politics was ensured during Adams' presidency. Adams faced his own vice president in his bid for reelection four years later, and America's first competitive electoral party system, which began to emerge in 1796, had arrived.

In 1800, Jefferson defeated Adams running along with Aaron Burr on the first formal party-endorsed ticket in the nation's history. Jefferson was elected president, and Burr his vice president. It is nearly impossible to overestimate the significance of this election in the history of the United States, its Democracy or its party politics. Here was a ruling faction being asked to relinquish power peacefully. Not since the Roman Republic gave way to dictatorship, had a political entity of any significance not relied on heredity or bloodshed to transition between rulers. States, regions or parties could potentially have ripped the young nation asunder. As was seen in the revolutions that followed America's Independence, the odds were not in the U.S.'s favor. We know, however, that America passed this crucial test. The Anti-Federalist won, and the Federalists went home. By the time Jefferson became president, however, the impact of the Federalists on the institutions and direction of the nation was broad, deep and enduring.

The Federalists drafted and secured the ratification of the Constitution that has governed the nation with minimal change for over 220 years. Hamilton's economic policies aided the United States in becoming the dominant economic power in the world today. The Washington Administration, working through the Treasury Department under Hamilton, assured sound finances for the nation and began putting in place an economic infrastructure that allowed the nation to take advantage of the sweeping economic opportunities presented by the Industrial Revolution. President Adams installed John Marshall as Chief Justice of the Supreme Court, guaranteeing a Federalist interpretation of the Constitution for more than three decades after the decline of national Federalist power. Most importantly, however, were the precedents set by Washington and Adams. Washington's voluntary two terms would not be surpassed until Franklin Delano Roosevelt assumed the office 136 years later; Adams's peaceful transfer of power likely spared the nation from a decent into totalitarianism or civil war. The blueprint for America's vacillation between leaders and parties was drawn. The rest of the story is which parties would influence this fluctuation, and how.

Upon his inauguration Jefferson declared, "[w]e are all Republicans; we are all Federalists." Jefferson was not holding out an olive branch to the recently defeated Federalists, but was declaring victory in the party wars of the previous two election cycles. The Republican dominance of national politics would last a generation, but eventually it, too, faced the same doctrinal divisions that imperiled the Federalists and impelled a realignment of the party politics of the nation.

Many argue that the Federalists under Adams failed to retain power because of a patrician attitude and sense of entitlement amongst many of the party's leaders. This is a recurring theme in American politics. Indeed the Republican reign ushered in by Jefferson ended against the backdrop of similar accusations against his party's entrenched power and elitism. A third party was the cause, and such movements have continued to affect and alter the nation's politics to the present.

The First Third:

The Anti-Masonic Party

It [*Freemasonry*] *is wrong – essentially wrong – a seed of evil, which can never produce any good.*

– John Quincy Adams, 1832

The Anti-Masonic Party emerged from the shadowy world of conspiracy and murder to become America's first literal "third" party. The party provides a useful starting point for the examination of third parties in the United States because, in addition to being first chronologically, the Anti-Masons exhibit traits of both Doctrinal and Realignment parties. A political outgrowth of diverse social and religious movements, the party reflected widespread hostility in the United States toward Freemasons, and all perceived secret and conspiratorial societies, in the public sphere. Though short-lived, the party made contributions to American politics that are visible and pervasive in the political milieu today.

Early Americans frowned upon secret societies of all kinds, viewing them as contrary to the democratic values upon which the nation was founded. Publications such as John Robinson's *Proofs of a Conspiracy Against All the Religions and Governments of Europe, carried on in the Secret Meetings of Free Masons, Illuminati, and Reading Societies*, and Abbé Augustin Barruel's translated *Mémoires pour servir à l'Histoire du Jacobinisme* equated societies such as the Freemasons and the Illuminati with anti-Christian crusaders responsible for the French Revolution and its Reign of Terror.

In 1798, in the midst of deep divisions between Federalists and Anti-Federalsists, Anglophiles and Francophiles, the prominent Massachusetts preacher, Jedidiah Morse, convinced that the United States was threatened by a Jacobine plot, delivered a sermon warning the young nation of these dangers. Morse's crusade was soon taken up throughout the churches of New England. Timothy Dwight, president of Yale University, and head of both Connecticut's Federalist Party and Congregational Church, also decried the supposed infiltration of Illuminati conspiracy into American society. Naturally, given Thomas Jefferson's Francophile leanings, Dwight easily alleged ties between the Democratic-Republicans and the perceived plots against America, going so far as to claim that Jacobine Anti-

Federalists instigated the Whiskey Rebellion.[6] In "The Duty of Americans in the Present Crisis," Dwight posited that

> [t]he sins of these enemies of Christ, and Christians, are of numbers and degrees which mock account and description. All that the malice and atheism of the Dragon, the cruelty and rapacity of the Beast, and the fraud and deceit of the false Prophet, can generate, or accomplish, swell the list ... Shall we introduce them into our government, our schools, our families? Shall our sons become the disciples of Voltaire ... or our daughters the concubines of the Illuminati?

Opposition to secret societies was firmly affixed in American religious movements and was slowly creeping into the political realm.

Though these outcries against conspiracy occurred a generation before the organized, political Anti-Masonry of the early 19th Century, the widespread conception of a vast, insidious conspiracy against America and its values is, as we shall see, an enduring feature of American society and its politics. The Anti-Masonic movement of the 1820s and 1830s fed on and extended this obsession into organized political action. What was needed was a target for this political urge, and a catalyst to unleash it. The target would be Freemasons in public office, and the catalyst would come in the form of the Morgan Affair.

In 1826, a bricklayer and former Freemason from Batavia, New York named William Morgan disappeared just as he was to publish an exposé of Masonic secrets. No connection between the disappearance and the Freemasons was ever proved. Nonetheless, critics of secret societies in general used the Morgan Affair to galvanize voters in the religiously fervent regions of the young nation. These so-called "burned-over" areas were so named because they were aflame with the

---

[6] The Whiskey Rebellion was one of the first great tests of the new national government. Viewed as a successful exercise of federal authority against the violent resistance to its laws, the Rebellion also helped to expose growing rifts between the Federalists and Anti-Federalists. Following Jefferson's election in 1800, the excise tax on whiskey that gave rise to the Rebellion was repealed.

passions of religious revivals, evangelism, and new religious and social movements. These regions were fertile ground for Anti-Masonic conspiracy as they were the same areas where the ideas of Morse and Dwight had been so widely accepted during the preceding generation.

In New York and New England, through the Appalachian regions of Kentucky and Tennessee, the Second Great Awakening of evangelical Protestantism was the response to the perceived secularism of the day. The Awakening stirred the spiritual and moral cores of many Americans, and gave impetus not only to the reaction against secret organizations, but also served to incubate reforming movements like abolition, temperance, pacifism, and women's rights. In turn, each of these reform movements became a significant social force in the story of America's third parties. Though the fury of the Awakening was directed at all perceived causes of the drift from strict religious observance, special attention was paid to secret societies.

By the end of the 18th century, many Americans no longer professed traditional Christian beliefs. At the same time, secret fraternal societies, such as the Freemasons, flourished throughout the country. The membership of these organizations largely consisted of middle- and upper-class white, Protestant men, often leading businessmen and politicians within their communities. The avowed purpose of groups like the Freemasons was to provide a forum for discussing the political issues of the day, as well as the moral self-improvement of their members. The secret rites and perceived elitism of these societies caused them to become favored targets of evangelical preachers of the period. Opposition to secret orders found an attentive audience amongst early Americans still burning with the egalitarian, democratic ideals of the revolution. Freemasons, however, were ubiquitous throughout the political elite and no party existed to address the social forces building in opposition to such secret societies.

30

Amidst the fear of anti-Christian/Anti-American conspiracy, Freemasons, if not Freemasonry, largely escaped direct political attack because several prominent Americans from the American Revolutionary generation were Masons. The Morgan Affair ended this exception and sparked a conflagration of anti-Masonry throughout the nation. Instantly, the Freemasons and their members were viewed by many as the greatest threat to Christendom and the country. Fear of Masonic control became rampant, and the ideas of the 1790s came rushing back into the public forum. The sentiment was summed up in a tract written by Charles Grandison Finney,[7] a prominent Revivalist Minister during the Second Great Awakening. Recalling the national mood at the time of the Morgan Affair in his 1869 book, *The Character, Claims and Practical Workings of Freemasonry*, Finney, a former third degree Master Mason, wrote that Freemasonry was

> highly injurious to the cause of Christ, and as eminently dangerous to the government of our country, and I suppose ... that nearly all the civil offices in the country were in the hands of Freemasons; and that the press was completely under their control, and almost altogether in their hands. Masons at that time boasted that all the civil offices in the country were in their hands ... I do not recollect a magistrate, or a constable, or sheriff ... that was not at that time a Freemason.

Mason influence was seen as a society-within-a-society, and outside its laws. Due to this perception, even before the Morgan Affair and the earlier conspiracy theories in the late 18th Century, Freemasonry was viewed with suspicion and fear.

Due in large part to the sometimes secretive nature of its rituals and activities, Freemasonry has long been suspected by religious institutions of engaging in subversive activities. The Catholic Church, itself ironically coupled with

---

[7] Finney is credited with coining the term "burned-over" to describe the areas in which the religious revivalism of the Second Great Awakening found fertile ground. In his autobiography, *Autobiography of Charles G. Finney* (1876), Finney states that no more fuel (potential converts) remained in the region to "burn" (convert).

Freemasons in denouncements of perceived threats to American values, felt particularly threatened by Freemasonry as both a competitor for membership and souls. Papal condemnation of Freemasonry came in 1738 from *Eminenti Apostolatus Specula* and again in 1884 in the encyclical *Humanum Genus*; the 1917 Code of Canon Law explicitly declares that joining Freemasonry entailed automatic excommunication. Additionally, the Eastern Orthodox Church forbade its members from becoming Masons. In vilifying Freemasonry, early 19th century American evangelical leaders were following in a long tradition of religious antagonism toward Masons.

While the precise origins of Freemasonry are lost to history, one widely-held theory maintains that Freemasonry was an institutional outgrowth of the medieval guilds of stonemasons. Another frequently expressed hypothesis holds that the Masons are direct descendants of the "Poor Fellow-Soldiers of Christ and the Temple of Solomon in Jerusalem" (more commonly known as "The Knights Templar"). Recorded Masonic history, however, dates to 14th century England with the formation of the London Masons Company in 1356.

The first recorded Freemason in America was John Skene, who emigrated from Scotland in 1682. By the mid-18th century, Masonic lodges were operating in most major communities in the 13 colonies and could count many famous American Revolutionaries as members. Benjamin Franklin, George Washington and Paul Revere were just a few of America's Revolutionary Masons. Many of the signers of the Declaration of Independence were Masons, as were one-third of the signers of the U.S. Constitution. Until the Morgan Affair, this famous membership shielded Masonry from outright hostility. However, such prominence also fueled the fire of conspiracy theorists, and the role of so many famous American Revolutionaries in the Freemasons was, for many, ample evidence of secret maneuverings to control the government. Religious and political leaders leapt upon the Morgan Affair to bring their fear of and disdain for Freemasonry to the fore of the national dialogue.

Freemasonry was, and remains, a favorite target of conspiracy theorists fearful of a Masonic New World Order either bent on world domination, or already secretly in control of global politics. In many democracies, Freemasonry has been accused of being a network where influence peddling and secret political dealings take place. In early America, with the untimely disappearance of William Morgan and the lack of response from the legal system and politicians alike, such fears appeared corroborated by fact. Thus was the stage set for a unified Anti-Masonic movement to take shape in America. Anti-Masonry rapidly evolved from a social and religious undercurrent to a political movement.

What really happened to Morgan is uncertain. After announcing he would publish a revelation of Masonic secrets, the head of the local Masonic lodge and numerous other Masons conspired to have Morgan arrested for an alleged debt. Their intent: pay his debt to secure his release, kidnap him, and imprison him in a U.S. fort near Niagara Falls. Morgan may have escaped from his imprisonment, but it seems more likely that the local Masons killed him.[8] The Masons involved in the kidnapping received light jail terms. Lodges did nothing to punish those responsible, and many powerful Masons, including prosecutors, judges, and legislators attempted to obscure the incident and obstruct justice, hoping the public furor would subside. It would not.

The perceived cover-up, and the popular belief that Masons held themselves above the law, combined to produce a huge public outcry against Freemasonry. Charges were leveled that Masonic secrecy was used to hide illegal and immoral activities, that Masonic oaths and initiations were unlawful and violent,

---

[8] This theory was given credibility when, in 1848, a man named Henry L. Valance allegedly confessed to his part in the murder.

and that Masons sought to subvert American political and religious institutions. Within a short time there were many who supported what they called the "Blessed Spirit" of fighting to abolish Freemasonry.

Since a purely religious movement could be only partially successful against Freemasonry, the movement quickly became political in order to unify opponents of Freemasonry. Numerous politicians and clergymen sincerely believed that the ideals of the United States and of Freemasonry were fundamentally in conflict and that the Masons were doing great harm to the country. Others viewed Anti-Masonry as a vehicle for their own political aspirations, particularly anti-Jacksonianism. Whatever the motives, religious and secular forces swiftly united under the banner of Anti-Masonry.

The Anti-Mason movement quickly grew beyond its original mission, with several politicians co-opting the Anti-Masonic movement as a means for organizing the various anti-Jacksonian forces throughout the United States. The overwhelming dominance of the Anti-Federalists and their political progeny, the Democratic-Republicans, was of great concern to many Americans. The election of Andrew Jackson, a Freemason, in 1828 amplified these feelings and led many to fear that Masons had taken control of the government. Single party rule by the Democratic-Republicans, stretching back to Thomas Jefferson, now with a personality cult centered on President Jackson, drove many to support Anti-Masonry as a bulwark against what they feared was the erosion of democracy in America. The Anti-Masonic Party hoped to capitalize on these feelings and the slowly disintegrating political strength once enjoyed by the Anti-Federalists.

President Jackson was an almost messianic figure to many Americans. His battlefield heroics and political resurrection fed this image. Jackson, the hero of New Orleans, was elected president in 1828 after losing to John Quincy Adams as a result of the so-called Corrupt Bargain four years earlier. Once in the White House,

Jackson's political and popular support seemed almost inexhaustible.   Political opportunists capitalized on the Morgan Affair and the Anti-Masonic passions it unleashed to rally to the Anti-Masonic banner as a means by which to challenge Jackson.

Anti-Masonic fervor found especially fertile ground in New York State. There, the Democratic-Republican political machine, known as the Albany Regency, was allied with Jackson.   The Regency was run by Martin Van Buren, who, like Jackson, was also a Mason.   Though perhaps only mildly sympathetic to Anti-Masonry, Van Buren's opponents, including New York's governor, DeWitt Clinton, used the Anti-Masonic movement to combat the Regency for political control.

Opposition to Van Buren's political establishment was led by William H. Seward and Thurlow Weed, staunch allies of Governor Clinton.   Seward and Weed turned to Anti-Masonry as a vehicle to continue their fight against Van Buren and the Regency.   Seward and Weed were perfect partners in pursuing their political aims.   They are responsible, in large part, for the speed and breadth of the spread of the Anti-Masonic Party.

William Seward's role in third party history is difficult to overestimate. Seward played a leading role in the formation and direction of the Whig, and Anti-Masonic parties, as well as the Republic Party and its predecessors.   Weed was a newspaperman, and with his help, Seward was elected to the New York State Senate as an Anti-Mason in 1830.   Four years later Seward ran for governor of New York as a Whig.   Though defeated in that contest he was victorious in the next governor's race.   In 1849 Seward was elected to the United States Senate as a Whig but joined the Republican Party after his reelection in 1855.   Seward eventually served as Secretary of State in President Lincoln's Republican administration in what Doris Kearns Goodwin has termed the "team of rivals" in her book by the same name.[9] Seward stayed on as Secretary of State when Johnson assumed the presidency and engineered "Seward's Folly," the purchase of Alaska from Russia in 1867.

Weed got his start at the influential *Albany Register*. While there he became an early supporter of DeWitt Clinton and an active Anti-Mason. Weed helped found New York's Anti-Masonic Society, a precursor to the New York State Anti-Masonic Party. Through the paper and his leadership of the Anti-Masons in New York, Weed came to wield substantial power in the state. This power was used not only to benefit the political aspirations of Seward and Weed's other friends. Weed, too, took to the campaign trail in New York.

In 1824, Weed was elected to the New York Assembly, and is credited with using his influence to deliver New York State to John Quincy Adams in his campaign for president that year.[10] The next year Weed purchased the *Rochester Telegraph*, but was quickly forced out by Masonic interests. In response Weed founded the *Antimasonic Enquirer*, which became the voice of Anti-Masonry in New York State. Following Weed's lead, the movement branched out nationally, using print to gain support. In just a few short years over 140 Anti-Masonic newspapers were in circulation in the United States. Anti-Masonic politics and media found little resistance to its spread as it filled a political vacuum left by the demise of the Federalists.

With the Federalists relegated to irrelevancy and fear of Masonic dominance over the Democratic-Republicans, Anti-Masons represented the only seemingly viable political alternative. In August of 1828, a resolution was adopted

---

[9] On the night of Lincoln's assassination, an attempt on Seward's life by co-conspirators of John Wilkes Booth was thwarted serendipitously by a neck-brace Seward wore in his sleep.

[10] Weed was also instrumental in the presidential nominations of William Henry Harrison (1840), Henry Clay (1844), Zachary Taylor (1848), Winfield Scott (1852), John Charles Frémont (1856) and Abraham Lincoln (1860).

by the New York Anti-Masonic Society pledging to "wholly disregard the two great political parties that at this time distract from the state of the Union ..." With this statement, New York's Anti-Masons declared themselves an alternate political party, America's first third party.

The Anti-Masonic Party grew quickly. The New York State Anti-Masonic Party was successful in electing local and statewide candidates and the party spread quickly into neighboring states. Already by 1828 the Anti-Masons were a political force of some significance in New York, controlling seventeen state assembly and four state senate seats. That year the New York Anti-Masonic Party nominated Soloman Southwick as its candidate for governor. Though he received widespread support Soloman failed to capture the governorship. In 1829, twenty-two Anti-Masonic candidates were elected to the New York State Assembly, and one candidate was elected to the State Senate.

While the ascendency of the Anti-Masons began in earnest in New York State in the 1820s, their golden age was felt nationally in the subsequent decade. During the 1830s, the Anti-Masonic Party held the governorship of Vermont and a majority in that state's legislature. The Anti-Masonic governor of Vermont, William A. Palmer, went on to win four consecutive elections. At one point during the decade, Massachusetts Anti-Masons held three seats in the state senate and controlled nearly one-third of the seats in the lower house of Massachusetts's legislature. In Pennsylvania, Anti-Masons took the governorship, sent a Congressman to Washington, D.C., and elected one state Senator and 15 state assemblymen. Despite this impressive electoral record, the Anti-Masonic claim to third party immortality rests not with any individual candidate or legislation, but with an idea. Two ideas actually.

In 1831, the Anti-Masons brought about an innovation in American politics, which today seems inextricable from national politics and political parties. In

Baltimore in that year, the Anti-Masonic Party held the first-ever national nominating convention of any political party. In the early nineteenth century, a party's presidential candidate was nominated by its congressional caucus. Since the Anti-Masonic Party had little congressional representation, they held a general meeting with 116 delegates from thirteen states. The delegates chose a nominee and discussed issues that formed the focus of their campaign. The issues championed by the Anti-Masons constituted the first-ever written party platform, spelling out, in addition to their opposition to secret societies, the party's position on the seminal social and political questions of the day.

At the party's convention, the Anti-Masons selected William Wirt as their presidential candidate. Wirt was an author, a lawyer and a statesman, who in 1817 wrote the biography entitled *Life and Character of Patrick Henry*. *Patrick Henry* contained the supposed text of Henry's most famous speeches, many of which had never been published. Some historians have speculated that some of Henry's most famous words, such as "Give me liberty or give me death!" were essentially fabricated by Wirt for this book.

In 1807, at the behest of President Thomas Jefferson, Wirt served as the prosecutor in the treason trial of Aaron Burr. Interestingly, Burr's famous conspiracy was alleged to have been concocted by Masons. Ten years later, President Monroe named Wirt to be United States Attorney General, a position he held until 1829. Wirt is credited with turning the position of U. S. Attorney General into one of great influence, and he began the practice of preserving his official opinions for use as precedents. As Attorney General, Wirt participated in some of the most important Supreme Court cases of his day, arguing over 170 cases before the High Court. Wirt participated in virtually every landmark case of the first third of the nineteenth century, including, *McCulloch v. Maryland* (1819),[11] *Gibbons* v. *Ogden* (1823),[12] and *Cherokee Nation v. Georgia* (1831).[13] Wirt argued many of these landmark cases with Daniel Webster, one of America's most celebrated orators.

Wirt also displayed an enlightened and idealistic view of justice and the law, taking on the advocacy of powerless groups against an unjust social order, something that hemmed with the egalitarian idealism of Anti-Masonic advocates. Wirt was described by Chief Justice Chase as "one of the purest and noblest of men." In 1821, Wirt defended nearly 300 African slaves in the case of the *Antelope*[14], a recaptured slave ship. Similar to the better-known case involving slaves aboard the *Amistad* [15]nineteen years later, the Africans of the *Antelope* represented by Wirt were freed and returned to West Africa, an astonishing feat for the time.

Immediately prior to becoming the Anti-Masonic presidential candidate in 1831, the Cherokee Nation sought Wirt as legal council during their attempt to gain recognition by the United States. This move was an effort to forestall machinations by the state of Georgia aimed at removing the Cherokees from the state. Wirt successfully defended the Cherokee Nation, but failed to have the Cherokees recognized as a sovereign nation. The high court ruled that the Cherokee Nation was a "distinct community" with self-government, "in which the laws of Georgia can have no force." The ruling established the doctrine that the federal government –

---

[11] 17 U.S. 316 (1819), also at 17 U.S. (4 Wheat.) 316; 4 L. Ed. 579.
[12] 22 U.S. 1 (1824), also at 22 U.S. (9 Wheat.) 1; 16 L. Ed. 23.
[13] 30 U.S. 1 (1831), also at 8 L. Ed. 25
[14] 23 U.S. 66 (1825), also at 10 U.S. (10 Wheat.) 66; 6 L. Ed. 268
[15] 40 U.S. 518 (1841), also at 40 U.S. (15 Pet.) 518; 10 L. Ed. 826

and not individual states – had authority over Native American affairs.[16] The *Cherokee* case was to be the last major act of William Wirt the U.S. Attorney General before his nomination.

Shortly after Wirt's nomination, the National Republicans adopted the convention model introduced by the Anti-Masons. The National Republicans chose Henry Clay to run for president and John Sergeant as his running mate. The following year the Democratic-Republicans held a convention as well in order to nominate Jackson for re-election. Though a *fait accompli* going into the gathering, the primary purpose of this convention was to demonstrate popular support for the president and allow Jackson to replace his vice president. During his first term Jackson regularly sparred with his vice president, John C. Calhoun, over political and personal matters. The obedient party man, Martin Van Buren, was tagged as Old Hickory's vice presidential candidate. With all three parties beginning the 1832 campaign with nominating conventions the institution became ingrained in the political process.

As the election got under way, Jackson vetoed a bill renewing the charter of the Second Bank of the United States, created in 1816 to help the Federal government deal with the debt and inflation caused by the War of 1812. However, it was actually Clay, believing it would split Jackson's support within the Democratic Party, who first brought the Bank into the 1832 campaign. Clay convinced Nicholas Biddle, president of the Bank, to apply for the Bank's re-charter in 1832, a full four years before the Bank's original mandate was set to expire. Congress was unable to marshal enough votes to override Jackson's veto. The re-authorization of the Bank

---

[16] In reaction to this decision, President Andrew Jackson has often been quoted as defying the Supreme Court with the words: "John Marshall has made his decision; now let him enforce it!" Jackson never actually said this; what Jackson did say was that "the decision of the Supreme Court has fell still born, and they find that they cannot coerce Georgia to yield to its mandate." Certainly the verbiage was of little import to the Cherokee Nation that was forced upon the aptly named "Trail of Tears" shortly thereafter.

and Jackson's veto of the same caused the Bank debate to swiftly eclipse all other matters in the 1832 election. With the National Bank and President Jackson's personality taking center stage in the 1832 election, the impact and influence of the Anti-Masonic Party ultimately waned.

Without Anti-Masonry as a central force in the 1832 campaign, Anti-Masons were barely distinguishable from National Republicans on most issues. Like the National Republicans, they supported a system of internal improvements and protective tariffs, favored the recharter of the Bank of the United States, supported indigenous rights and were outraged by Jackson's support of Georgia's Cherokee policy in the face of the Supreme Court's ruling favoring the Cherokees. Unlike the National Republicans, though, the Anti-Mason leaders often championed women's rights.

The true difference between the Anti-Masons and the National Republicans, however, lay in the fact that the Anti-Masons were generally antislavery teetotalers. This distinction over slavery and alcohol was due in large part to the religious base of Anti-Mason support, which also formed the foundation of abolitionist and prohibitionist third parties in 19th century America. Not surprisingly, aversion to alcohol and an abhorrence of the institution of slavery formed the nuclei of latter-day third parties in America. Clay, on the other hand, was a slave-owning Mason, who dueled and drank. These differences were seen at the time to be mainly superficial. In the end, such differences were not enough to prevent many supporters of the Anti-Masons from drifting to the National Republicans as they embraced much of the Anti-Masonic Party platform. As the National Republicans adopted many of the Anti-Masonic platform planks, many Anti-Masonic voters adopted the National Republican Party.

Throughout American history burgeoning social and political movements have seen their initial popularity usurped by more well-established parties. Though the National Republicans never took up the mantle of Anti-Masonry, the two parties shared many Anti-Jacksonian positions with respect to matters of economics and federalism. As the Anti-Masonic Party expanded, it came to be dominated by new members more inspired by personal ambition or by a general opposition to the Jacksonian Democrats than by Anti-Masonry. In the years following the election of 1832 many Anti-Masons joined with the National Republicans, ultimately going on to form the Whig Party, and later the Republican Partiy and its predecessors. These voters and their myriad parties had to wait nearly three decades, though, to enjoy electoral success.

It was clear long before Election Day that Jackson would triumph. Jackson and Van Buren defeated Clay and Sergeant handily, winning by a margin of more than 150,000 popular votes and 170 votes in the Electoral College. Wirt picked up just over 100,000 votes, about seven percent of the total, and took Vermont's seven electoral votes. Though the party made a respectable showing, Wirt's candidacy did not advance the Anti-Masonic cause. Ironically, and highly damaging to the image of the party, news emerged that Wirt was a Mason who had not repudiated his connection with the order. Wirt's speech at the Anti-Masonic convention, defending the organization his party sought to eradicate, effectively demolished his value as a candidate.

By the time it was all over, fears of Jackson's political dominance and the Bank debate, along with the ever-present issue of slavery, became the fault lines of American politics. Following the election of 1832, Wirt summed up the feelings of disheartened Anti-Masons and National Republicans alike: "My opinion, is that [Jackson] may be President for life if he chooses." Within a decade, the Anti-Masonic Party disappeared from the political scene.

Anti-Masonry nonetheless left an indelible imprint on American political culture and was, at least briefly, highly successful in its social and political aims.

The nominating convention established norms and rituals that persist. Nominating conventions have become forums to promote party unity, lambaste the opposition, and set the tone for the substance of the party's platform. The Anti-Masonic movement, which remained centered in Western New York, achieved its principal goal: by 1835 there were only 49 lodges with 3,000 members in New York State, down from 480 lodges with 20,000 members ten years earlier. Connecticut saw half its lodges close their doors, and in Maine Freemasonry virtually ceased to exist. Following the dissolution of the Anti-Masonic Party, however, American Freemasonry was restored. On the eve of the Civil War, Masonry was once again as widespread as before the Morgan Affair, and nearly a third of the presidents since Jackson have been Freemasons.

At its height the Anti-Masonic Party held at least twenty-five seats in the U.S. House of Representatives, more than 10 percent of House seats at the time. The last Anti-Masons served in the U.S. Congress until 1841. Social Anti-Masonry survived far beyond the dissolution of the Anti-Masonic Party. In 1882, a large monument to William Morgan was placed by Anti-Masons in the Batavia City Cemetery. It reads:

> Sacred to the memory of Wm. Morgan, a native of Virginia, a Capt. in the War of 1812, a respectable citizen of Batavia, and a martyr to the freedom of writing, printing and speaking the truth. He was abducted from near this spot in the year 1826, by Freemasons and murdered for revealing the secrets of their order. The court records of Genesee County, and the files of the Batavia Advocate, kept in the Recorders office contain the history of the events that caused the erection of this monument.

This gesture, however, was no more than the last gasp of organized Anti-Masonry within the United States.

Regardless of how Anti-Masonic success is measured, the Anti-Masonic Party illustrates the first successful effort by religious groups to organize politically. Like abolitionists in subsequent decades and the Prohibition Party a half-century later, the Anti-Masonic Party demonstrated how religious fervor could be mobilized to political action. More importantly, the Anti-Masons showed that a single-issue party could engage in the broader political discourse. The harnessing of narrow socio-religious energy for broader political action, and resistance to perceived elite dominance of the political system is a recurrent theme in American history and central to third party history. As such, it forms much of the Anti-Masonic Party's tremendous legacy for third parties.

Political Anti-Masonry did not merely respond to social forces and a political vacuum. The party pioneered the popular party-nominating convention for local, state, and federal offices — an innovation soon imitated by the National Republicans and Democratic-Republicans and now a permanent fixture of American politics. It was the first formal party to take advantage of technological advances in communication and transportation — there were 141 Anti-Masonic papers in 1832, originating from 15 states and Anti-Masonic leaders traveled widely to campaign and lecture. Yet Anti-Masonry's primary contribution lies in the phenomenon itself in terms of party politics, voter mobilization, and political culture – the Anti-Masonic Party reinvented the way politics are conducted in the United States. In addition, the essentially one-issue platform of the Anti-Masonic Party, and its moderate political success established a legacy for future Doctrinal third parties to follow.

While clearly Doctrinal at its core, the Anti-Masonic party can be labeled as both a Realignment and a Doctrinal party. Like all future Doctrinal incarnations, the Anti-Masonic Party was created for a single purpose: the eradication of fraternal, secret societies within the United States. As one of the causes of the end of America's only period of one-party rule, the Anti-Masonic Party realigned American politics and provided the opportunity for future political parties to emerge.

The Anti-Masons further provide an excellent launching point for the exploration of American third party history for their embodiment and embrace of a recurring socio-political phenomenon in America. As has been noted, the Anti-Masonic Party took as its rallying cry a call for the elimination of Freemasons from public life. The rejection of elitism or entrenched interests forms the basis of many third parties explored in this work. The Anti-Masons fed on the pervasive fear of conspiracy against America. The call to arms of one group against another, especially in the context of some perceived threat to American society and American values, whether passive or coordinated, is echoed throughout American history. Whether advocating prohibition or racial discrimination, American history is littered with intolerance of one form or another that found political voice, but the Anti-Masons were the first.

Life ... *Liberty?* ... and the Pursuit of Happiness – Abolitionist Parties: Liberty & Free Soil

" ... no other party in the country represents the true principles of American liberty, or the true spirit of the Constitution of the United States."

– 1844 Liberty Party Platform

The sin of slavery, and its legacy, has shaped America more than any other factor in its history. From the compromises sought in drafting the Constitution through the outbreak of the Civil War, to the Civil Rights movement and the debate over Affirmative Action, the lingering effects of this loathsome chapter in American history continue to affect American culture and politics to this day, including the significance of the election of America's first black president. It is in reaction to this reprehensible practice that the Liberty and Free Soil parties were formed.

Clearly the Liberty party, and its progeny, the Free Soil Party, represent the very best of Doctrinal party politics. However, in marked contrast to ephemeral and fringe doctrinal parties, the Liberty Party was the catalyst behind the greatest realignment in U.S. history – the Liberty Party begot the Free Soil Party, which begot the Republican Party, the only example in American history of a third party achieving major party status, where it remains to this day.

During the Constitutional Convention and the early days of the republic, myriad issues drew the attention of the electorate and the political class. Each question the Founders confronted greatly affected the evolution of the country as the new nation sought to define itself. However, while foreign relations and economic matters are the typical focus of statecraft, a uniquely troubling question at the founding of the United States was slavery.

The Three-Fifths Compromise during the 1787 Constitutional Convention was an agreement between southern and northern states in which three-fifths of the slave population were to be counted for census purposes regarding both the distribution of taxes and the apportionment of representatives to the Congress. Without this provision it is unlikely the Constitution would have been adopted and ratified, and the fledgling nation would have been stillborn. The practical effect of this repugnant exercise in political expediency was that southern states dominated national politics in the years from the founding of the nation until the period immediately prior to the Civil War.

As the nation grew and developed, numerous measures were adopted to postpone or prevent a final reckoning over the issue of slavery. Many of these actions, which undoubtedly delayed purging the cancer of slavery from the national corpus, were only possible due to the disproportionate representation of slaveholding states in the House of Representatives and the Electoral College. For example, in 1793 slave states would have been apportioned 33 seats in the House of Representatives had the seats been assigned based exclusively on the free, voting population rather than permitting the inclusion of three-fifths of the non-voting slave population for this calculus; instead they were apportioned 47 seats chosen exclusively by whites. In 1812, slaveholding states controlled 76 seats instead of 59; in 1833, they had 98 instead of 73. As a result, southerners dominated the Presidency, the Speakership of the House, and the Supreme Court, and it is hard to imagine how Thomas Jefferson would have won the presidency in 1800 without the aid of the Three-Fifths Compromise and the political advantage it created.

Historians have postulated that the Missouri Compromise and the Kansas-Nebraska Act, attempts to balance the irreconcilable differences in the slavery debate, would not have been possible without the outsized legislative and electoral strength of the pro-slavery South. The infamous *Dred Scot* [17]decision and the odious Fugitive Slave Acts, were heavy-handed moves by a slave-holding dominated ruling class that regularly threatened dissolution of the union should their demands not be met. However, postponing civil war did not prevent it and countless black Americans continued to languish in bondage in the decades following America's independence.

---

[17] 60 U.S. 393 (1857), see also 60 U.S. (19 Howard) 393; 15 L. Ed. 691

The compromises reached to forge and maintain the union did not mute the opponents of slavery. Social opposition to slavery grew and the body politic became ever more polarized. The forces aligned against slavery needed to coalesce to combat this evil. As with all things American, this battle was brought to the ballot. Without this political focus on abolition, the enshrined systemic advantage afforded the pro-slavery forces would be nearly impossible to combat.

The Liberty Party became the first abolitionist party in America. The party's formation represented the culmination of a decade of heightening abolitionist social and political activity in the nation. The party also sought to fill the void left by the major parties of the time, the Democrats and the Whigs, whose confused platforms all but ignored the issue of slavery. With slavery, and its antipode, abolition, debated vociferously since the nation's birth, this vacuum demanded to be filled. However, from its inception, political abolition struggled to define itself. Would the movement remain one of doctrinaire protest, or would it seek full political engagement, thus requiring a complete platform and broader appeal?

Serious debate over abolition took place throughout the nation in the generation following the American Revolution. North and South sought solutions compatible with their ideologies and palpable to their constituents. In the Virginia legislature in 1829 and 1831 abolition itself was debated. In the North, and supported by Virginian President James Monroe, discussion began about the possibility of freeing the slaves and resettling them back in Africa.[18]

Social friction over slavery increased as solutions appeared ever more elusive. With the publication of David Walker's *Appeal to the Colored Citizens of the World* in 1829 and Nat Turner's slave rebellion in 1831, Southerners reacted with

---

[18] This proposal led to the founding of Liberia, whose capital, Monrovia, is named for President Monroe.

alarm at what they saw as a threat to their way of life. Southern anxiety only increased further with the founding of the American Anti-Slavery Society in Philadelphia, a proto-political movement that would lead to the formation of the abolitionist Liberty and Free Soil political parties.

In 1831 William Lloyd Garrison began publishing *The Liberator*, whose mast head read, "I am in earnest – I will not equivocate – I will not excuse – I will not retreat a single inch – **and I will be heard.**" Two years later the brothers Arthur and Lewis Tappan, along with Garrison, organized the American Anti-Slavery Society. The organization quickly grew, and when, two years later, it became a national organization, Arthur Tappan was elected its first president. Garrison, however, soon emerged as the main figure in the organization, much to the dismay of members who objected to his radical views and management style – Garrison reserved some of his most vocal criticism for moderate abolitionists. The Anti-Slavery Society organized meetings, arranged the signing of petitions, printed and distributed anti-slavery materials, and employed people to go on lecture tours of the United States. By the end of the decade the society had 250,000 members in 2,000 local chapters, and published more than twenty journals.

The Society's membership included many of the great leaders in America's fight for social justice, including Fredrick Douglass, Susan B. Anthony and Elizabeth Cady Stanton. Anthony and Stanton's prominence in the organization, and the role of women in general, caused friction between those who, curiously, believed that female leadership was too radical in a movement dedicated to abolition. Garrison's domineering management style did not help to sooth impassioned feelings over this and other disagreements amongst Society leadership that eventually led to schism in the movement.

The Society was the scene of many disputes between radical reformers like Garrison and others who advocated a more moderate approach to the issue of

50

slavery. One great difference between the two camps was whether abolitionists should enter politics as a distinct party. Some members of the Anti-Slavery Society considered the organization to be too radical, and they objected to Garrison's militant attacks on the Constitution (Garrison once burned a copy on the Fourth of July, proclaiming "so perish all compromises with tyranny"). Leaders such as Garrison and Douglass were as committed to women's rights as they were to the abolition of slavery. Others, such as the Arthur Tappan and James Birney, a former slave-holder who came to support the Liberia plan and went on to become the Liberty Party's candidate in 1840 and 1844, sought a more tempered approach focused solely on the issue of abolition.

Tappan and Birney left the Anti-Slavery Society and formed a rival organization, the American and Foreign Anti-Slavery Society, at a state convention in Warsaw, New York in 1839, with other anti-feminist abolitionists. This new organization refused to support the woman's rights movement and instead concentrated exclusively on the subject of slavery. On April 1 of the following year, at a national convention in Albany, New York, delegates from six states officially adopted the name Liberty Party, nominated Birney as its presidential candidate, and declared abolition of slavery to be the sole plank in the party's platform.

In the ensuing 1840 election Birney ran with Thomas Earle, a former delegate to revise Pennsylvania's State Constitution who called for extending suffrage to African Americans. The intense electioneering of 1840 generated an unprecedented turnout: nearly 80 percent of the electorate voted, up from 58 percent in 1836. The race was tight in every region of the nation, but the Whigs carried the election. Harrison outpolled Van Buren by a popular vote of 1,275,612 to 1,130,033. James Birney and the Liberty Party won only 7,053 votes, barely one-third of one percent. Despite these disappointing results, the Liberty Party remained active and worked at the state and local level to build the party.

Following the 1840 election, the Liberty Party gained recruits and newspaper support and was becoming a threat to the two major parties in close northern states, where it aimed to swing the balance of power. Birney was nominated again in November 1844 and ran with Thomas Morris, a Democratic Senator from Ohio, polling 62,300 votes. Birney and the Liberty Party's electoral showing hurt Henry Clay's prospects and tipped the election in favor of Democrat James K. Polk, who supported the annexation of Texas and the extension of slavery to the newly acquired territory.[19] In voting for abolition, Liberty Party supporters had all but guaranteed the strengthening and expansion of the practice of slavery in the nation.

This unintended consequence should be familiar to observers and students of the campaign of Green Party candidate Ralph Nader in 2000. Without the votes of Nader supporters, Democratic Vice President Albert Gore lost Florida and with it the election;[20] these voters, who supported the ultra-leftist Green Party candidate ultimately handed the election to the less desirable (in their eyes) of Nader's opponents, Republican George W. Bush. While Nader supporters cast their vote for various reasons, certainly no Green Party supporter intended to hand the presidency to an oilman from Texas whose environmental policy was, to put it mildly, not something most environmentalists viewed with much enthusiasm. Such outcomes are the ever-looming risk for third parties and present one of the greatest obstacles to their growth. The moment a third party candidate is viewed as a spoiler, the portion of the electorate previously willing to cast a vote for third parties quickly loses its appetite for such experimentation. Ralph Nader's vote fell

---

[19] A third Tappan brother, Ohio Senator Benjamin Tappan, was censured by the Senate for disclosing the terms of a secret communiqué between President Taylor and the New York Evening Post regarding the terms of the annexation of Texas.

[20] As shall be seen, the impact of Nader, and another third party candidate, Patrick Buchanan, were felt in numerous states, though Florida will forever be the iconic state of third party politics in the 2000 presidential election.

from over 2.8 million, or 2.7% of votes cast in the 2000 elections, to less than half a million, or 0.38%, four years later. Such a fate would befall the Liberty Party as well.

In 1848, Salmon P. Chase, head of the Liberty Party in Ohio, presided over a convention in Buffalo, New York that joined the Liberty Party with so-called *Barnburner* Democrats from New York to form the Free Soil Party. Although the Liberty Party nominated John P. Hale and Leicester King to run in that year's election, party leaders urged the members to vote for candidates of the newly organized Free Soil Party; as such, Hale withdrew his candidacy. The abolitionist torch was thus passed from the fiercely doctrinal Liberty Party to the more moderate Free Soil Party.

The Free Soil candidate in 1848 was former Democratic president Martin Van Buren. Van Buren ran with Charles Francis Adams, the son and grandson of former presidents John and John Quincy Adams. Many Free Soilers had grave reservations about the Van Buren candidacy. While in office Van Buren had vowed to veto any bill abolishing slavery in the District of Columbia without the approval of both Virginia and Maryland. In seeking to rally support around Van Buren, Charles Sumner proclaimed that "it is not for the Van Buren of 1838 we are to vote, but for the Van Buren of today." Charles Sumner would later join the U.S. Senate following a special election; he was an ardent opponent of slavery and the Compromises of the 1850s, which ultimately led to an infamous and brutal attack on Sumner by Congressman Preston Brooks on the floor of Senate. While denouncing the Kansas-Nebraska Act in his "Crime Against Kansas" speech, Sumner attacked the authors of the act, including Andrew Butler of South Carolina, Brooks' mentor and uncle. Sumner's speech, which mockingly alluded to Butler's speech impediment after a stroke, also stated that Butler had taken "a mistress ..., who, though ugly to others, is always lovely to him; though polluted in the sight of the world, is chaste in his sight – I mean, the harlot, Slavery." Two days later, Brooks arrived at Sumner's office and beat Sumner senseless, stopping only after his cane shattered from the repeated blows.

Though Van Buren and Adams joined the race a mere three months before the elections, they polled surprisingly well, winning more than 10% of the popular vote (though failing to gain a single electoral vote). The Free Soil party also managed to capture 16 seats in Congress and was able to exercise power in great excess of their numbers by essentially tipping (and, ultimately, controlling) the balance of power in both chambers.

The national vote between Whig Zachary Taylor and Democrat Lewis Cass was close. Taylor won by 36 electoral votes (163 to 127), the exact number of electoral votes cast by New York's delegation in that election. The abolitionists, now in the guise of the Free Soil Party, had yet again affected the balance of power in New York State and through it the national election; only this time the election was tipped to the Whigs. Taylor proved to be a strong opponent of the expansion of slavery and the Compromise of 1850. Nevertheless, when President Taylor died during the Compromise debates his successor, Millard Fillmore, took the side of the Compromises' proponents.

Despite the 1848 election victory, the Taylor/Fillmore administration marked the beginning of the end for the Whig Party. The Compromise of 1850 and the abrupt shift from opposition to the Compromises under Taylor to support of the Compromises under Fillmore exposed the stark division within the party. The flight of the Barnburners had severely weakened the Whigs and the split between pro- and anti-slavery factions proved irreparable.

By the 1852 election, the leadership of the Whig Party had shifted. Henry Clay, one of the architects of the Compromise of 1850, and the great orator Daniel Webster, also a supporter of the Compromise to ensure survival of the union, had died. In their place were Senator William H. Seward and Representative Thaddeus Stevens. Seward had supported Taylor in the 1848 election and while in the Senate opposed the Compromise of 1850. Stevens was elected to the House in 1848 and was a staunch opponent of what he considered a conspiracy by pro-slave interests to seize control of the federal government. Seward was also an active participant in the Underground Railroad. With the replacement of Clay and Webster with Seward and Stevens, support for the Whigs in the South utterly collapsed.

With the shift in Whig leadership and the loss of the South, the time was ripe for the Whigs to adopt abolition firmly in their platform and absorb the Free Soilers and the remaining adherents to the Liberty Party. As with past doctrinal parties it appeared the abolitionists would be absorbed into a major party. But this did not happen. The Free Soil Party nominated John P. Hale, the 1848 Liberty Party candidate who had withdrawn that year in the face of the Free Soil challenge. Despite their representation in the U.S. Congress, and the failure of the Whigs to forge a coalition with the abolitionists, Hale's candidacy was to be the Free Soil Party's last.

The Free Soil party, though it ceased to formally exist, was not absorbed by the Whig Party in the next election cycle. The Whig Party continued its decline. Eventually debate over the Kansas-Nebraska Act, which sought to replace the Missouri Compromise of 1820 and the Compromise of 1850 with a measure that would open new western territory to popular sovereignty – leaving the question of slavery to voters in these territories – ripped the Whig Party asunder. In Ottawa, Illinois, in August, 1854, an alliance was brokered between the Free Soil Party and the Whigs that gave rise to the Republican Party. Shortly thereafter the Kansas-Nebraska Act's main author, Illinois Democratic Senator Stephen Douglas, engaged in a debate with fellow Illinoisan, Abraham Lincoln. Lincoln exclaimed that the Kansas-Nebraska Act *declared* indifference, but as I must think, covert *real* zeal for the spread of slavery, I cannot but hate it. I hate it because of the monstrous injustice of slavery itself. I hate it because it deprives our republican example of its just influence in the world — enables the enemies of free institutions, with plausibility, to taunt us as hypocrites — causes the real friends of freedom to doubt our sincerity, and especially because it forces so many really good men amongst ourselves into an open war with the very fundamental principles of civil liberty — criticizing the Declaration of Independence, and insisting that there is no right principle of action but *self-interest.*

Abolition had arrived in the form of a major, albeit new, party. The realignment – a realignment born of doctrinal third party politics – was complete.

Though the Free Soil Party no longer existed, the Republican Party slogan shows that their legacy lived on. John C. Frémont ran as the first Republican nominee for President in 1856; the party called for "free soil, free labor, free speech, free men, Frémont." The doctrinal third party politics of abolition, which evolved and grew as the mantle passed from the Liberty Party to the Free Soil Party and then, ultimately, to the Republican Party, caused realignment in the American political system not seen before or since. The result of this realignment was nothing less than the wholesale reconstitution of the very structure of America.

In 1858, Lincoln and Douglas faced each other in a series of debates as the men challenged each other for a seat in the United States Senate. Douglas won that election, but when the two faced off again two years later in the 1860 presidential campaign, Lincoln was the victor. The Republican Party, enjoying the earlier efforts of the Liberty and Free Soil Parties, and the implosion of the Whigs, had, in six short years, gone from third party offspring to placing their candidate in the White House.[21] They were a third party no more.

---

[21] Further discussion of the Republican Party once Lincoln ascended to the presidency has no place in a book on third parties, though the role of the party during and after the American Civil War straight through to the present is fascinating reading indeed.

All (White, Anglo-Saxon, Protestant) Men are Created Equal:

The American Know Nothings

Americans must rule America

- 1856 Platform of the Know Nothing Party

Just as the Whigs were disintegrating and providing political space for the rise of the Republican Party, several other political movements appeared on America's political landscape in the decades leading up to the Civil War. In stark contrast to the embracing and progressive Liberty and Free Soil Parties, the Know Nothing Party arose to limit America's political participation. Called the Know Nothings because followers were advised to respond "I know nothing" when asked about the group, the party's emergence in American politics is rooted firmly in two recurring American themes: xenophobia and paranoia. That being the case, the group makes an informative study in the rise and fall of movements grounded in ephemeral causes - here, a rabid fear of rising immigration rolls.

By the 1840s, immigration to the young republic had gained tremendous momentum. Between 1846 and 1855, three million immigrants arrived on American soil eager to seize and define the inchoate American dream. The new country was hungry for the energetic, driven individuals, people willing to brave a transatlantic trek in search of opportunity. Homestead laws creating favorable conditions for those ready to tame the wild frontier were especially appealing. Whereas a landless peasant in Europe would ever remain a landless peasant in Europe, here was the opportunity to take, work, and actually *own* a sizeable patch of verdant land. Immigrants from all corners of Europe emigrated in the hope of attaining the religious freedom, and social and economic mobility associated with the young republic. In America, they found a nation whose success would be intertwined with their own. However, not all Americans were prepared to accept the huddled masses into the body politic. Many, then as now, regarded the incoming immigrants with a nebulous mix of fear and disdain. A litany of prominent Americans began questioning their motives, and, in time, their loyalty.

Oddly enough, one of the party's patriarchs was none other Samuel F. B. Morse. The "American Leonardo" drew heavily on his scientific cachet to lead the campaign against Catholics. Having learned that an Austrian group called the Leopoldine Society to Aid the Missions was making contributions to the bishop of Cincinnati to build churches and schools for Catholics, Morse immediately suspected a papal conspiracy was afoot to establish a "new Vatican" in – oddest of all places – Ohio. In language that could have easily come from the earlier writings of Anti-Masons, Morse penned a series of widely-read articles urging Protestant unity against the Catholic establishment, warning portentously that "the ratio of increase of Popery is the exact ratio of decrease of civil liberty."

In 1835, Morse published what would inevitably become part of the Know Nothing canon: a lengthy diatribe entitled *Foreign Conspiracies against the Liberties of the United States*. "A conspiracy exists," the celebrated painter and scientist proclaimed. "Its plans are already in operation ... we are attacked in a vulnerable quarter which cannot be defended by our ships, our forts, or our armies." Though Catholicism was naturally concentrated in the Vatican, Morse saw logistical coordination – and Catholic power – emanating from Vienna: "Austria is now acting in this country. She has devised a grand scheme. She has organized a great plan for doing something here ... she has her Jesuit missionaries traveling through the land; she has supplied them with money, and has furnished a fountain for a regular supply."

In the first book to connect the flood of foreign immigrants into eastern ports with a Vatican plot for global conquest, Morse cautioned vigilant Americans that if America failed to protect itself from the Vatican plot, it would be no time before "some scion of the House of Hapsburg would be installed as Emperor of the United States." Seeking to reap the fruits of his own alarmism, Morse accepted a nomination from New York's Native American Democratic Association – a Know Nothing affiliate – to run for the New York mayoralty shortly after the publication of *Foreign Conspiracies*. Though he received fewer than fifteen hundred votes, his limited success was an augur of the Know Nothings' coming victories. While Morse is remembered primarily as the father of the telegraph and modern communications, his ardent spokesmanship for the Know Nothings – and later, pro-slavery forces – tarnishes his legacy deeply.

Another prominent ally in the Know Nothing cause was Lyman Beecher, a seventh-generation Puritan preacher and the father of Harriet Beecher Stowe. Beecher followed Morse's seminal *Foreign Conspiracies* with his own tract, earnestly entitled *Plea for the West*. Beecher's text was remarkable in that it expanded on, and added texture to Morse's suspected papal plot. Replete with admonitory language, which would be typical of later Know Nothing pamphlets, the screed intertwined the fate of the young Republic with the Catholic "settlement of the West." "Mighty causes," Beecher began, "like floods from distant mountains, are rushing with accumulating power, to their consummation of good or evil, and soon our character and destiny will be stereotyped forever." "It is equally plain," he prophesied, "that the religious and political destiny of our nation is to be decided in the West."

Citing a travelogue from a visitor to Austria, Beecher paints for the reader a dire specter of the Catholic myrmidons: "And what are the people of Austria? They are slaves, slaves in body and mind, whipped and disciplined by priests to have no opinion of their own, and taught to consider their emperor their God." In one of his most impassioned passages, Beecher impressed upon the reader the conviction that Catholicism was the most dire threat the nation faced:

> ...the Catholicity of this nation, and its rapid increase, cannot be safely regarded as a mere insulated religion, but rather as one department of a comprehensive effort to maintain despotic government against the march of free institutions, by an invigorated union of ecclesiastical and political power; and though the Catholics among us may, as a body, be unapprised [sic] of this policy, and ought not to be reviled, or denounced, or

61

falsely accused, or assailed by rumor, and invidious epithets, neither are they to be unwatched, or entrusted with the education of the nation, or the balance of her suffrage ... There is no denomination but the Catholic which acknowledges implicit subjection to the spiritual dominion of a foreign prince in whom the church and state are united, and whose political relations modify, by the intrigues of the European powers, his ecclesiastical decisions -- a prince dependent on the protection, and under the control of one of the most despotic governments of Europe. There is no church but the Catholic in our land which claims infallibility, and the right of a universal spiritual jurisdiction, and makes heresy a capital offence ... Whatever we do, it must be done quickly; for there is a tide in human things which waits not,- moments on which the destiny of a nation balances ...

Whereas Morse was satisfied making the straightforward argument that Catholics were to be denied suffrage, citizenship, and even entry into American ports because of a general allegiance to a "foreign Prince," Beecher purported to reveal the precise nature of the Catholic plot: a purported Austrian-Vatican axis to send hordes of Catholic immigrants into the great, untamed West, populate the region and vote as they were told.

The American frontier was to be the American Armageddon, or, as historian Richard Hofstadter observed, it was in the West that "Protestantism was engaged in a life-or-death struggle with Catholicism." A decade later, Protestant meetings were held in Philadelphia to discuss Beecher's ideas and address the perceived Catholic threat generally. The mood surrounding the meetings became so heated that several riots broke out, resulting in 13 deaths, hundreds of injuries, two Catholic churches being destroyed along with hundreds of homes. Sadly, the riots presaged the violent nature of the anti-Catholic unrest that defined the following decade.

A third book emerged a year after Morse and Beecher's publications. Arguably the most widely read book of its time in the United States before *Uncle*

Tom's Cabin, a book by the title _Awful Disclosures of the Hotel Dieu Nunnery of Montreal,_ supposedly written by Maria Monk, surfaced early in 1836. The author, who claimed to have escaped from a Montreal convent after five years there as novice and nun, reported life inside the nunnery in tremendous, lurid detail. Among the more scandalous reports, the author recounted being told by the Mother Superior to "obey the priests in all things" upon hearing "the shrieks of the helpless women in the hands of wicked men" in the halls of the convent. Monk described her discovery of countless hidden tunnels, prisons, and eventually, to her "utter astonishment and horror," mass graves. The extent of her obedience was to be absolute, as it was soon revealed that numerous infants born of convent liaisons were baptized and immediately slain so that they might ascend at once to heaven. Her book, hotly attacked and almost immediately discredited as a fabrication, continued to be read and believed long after Monk's mother revealed her daughter was somewhat psychologically "addled" from a childhood accident. Though Maria Monk would die in prison, reportedly jailed for pickpocketing a client in a brothel, her sordid convent tales only fueled the belief that Catholicism was little more than a parlous, pernicious ideology bent on domination and subjugation.

The Know Nothings' actual genesis and subsequent success depended heavily on an intoxicating cocktail of growing national confidence mixed with fear of the other stoked by influential figures of the day. Almost divinely situated on a landmass insulated from regular continental wars and plagues, the young republic steadily forged its identity under curious but skeptical European eyes. In time, manifest destiny coalesced with the gradual realization of America's true potential: to surpass its war-weary neighbors across the Atlantic as the world's greatest nation.

Ever more self-assured with their young nation's accomplishments, the new Native Americans (as distinguished from indigenous, actual Native Americans) became more guarded with their treasures. In time, the question Morse and Beecher had posed spread: Why, indeed, should America's star-writ bounty be shared with – or jeopardized by – immigrants who served foreign influences? Over the course of a single generation, the country that had systematically endeavored to fill its vast and largely empty landmass with anyone intrepid (or foolish) enough to do so, began to feel the first pangs of insularity. Prominent journalists and thinkers seemed in agreement and helped to give momentum to the intensifying and self-reinforcing cycle of nationalism and xenophobia.

Horace Bushnell, one of the founders of liberal Protestantism in the United States, declared "Our first danger is barbarism, Romanism next." Newspaperman Horace Greeley conceded in the *New York Tribune*, which he had helped found in 1841, that many immigrants were "deplorably clannish, misguided, and prone to violence." However, reflecting upon the Know Nothing mantra, he demanded of his readers "How can we regard any movement of this sort as other than hostile to the vital principles of our Republic?" Greeley was ideally situated to comment on the Nativist controversies: for many, New York City was the epicenter of the Nativist movement. The city, then and now a natural immigration hub, saw a burgeoning foreign population as early as 1828. After Morse's abortive mayoral bid in 1835, the victorious Democrats and opposition Whigs chose to further alienate the Nativist minority by doling out local offices to each other, giving the lion's share to foreign born citizens toeing the party lines.

Worries over the mounting tide of immigrants, primarily composed of Germans in the Midwest and Irish along the Eastern seaboard, came to dominate press coverage. As early as 1825, nearly 40% of all periodicals published in the United States expressed anti-immigrant or anti-Catholic rhetoric, with some of the more popular rags bearing such titles as *The Protestant Vindicator*, and *The Downfall of Babylon*. Sensing danger to God and country alike, community leaders sought to band together to combat devious foreign influences, particularly the "evil of Popery." Indeed, as Beecher had said time and again, the most dangerous foreign influence of all was Pope Gregory XVI. That most of the new immigrants were Roman Catholic was hardly comforting to the overwhelmingly Protestant population. The perceived duality of allegiance – to a "foreign prince" on the one hand, and supposedly to America on the other – was reason enough, many argued, to exclude Roman Catholics from participating in the American experiment, including denying citizenship altogether.

The fears of Catholics in the United States and concerns about their loyalties dates from its founding and lasted well into the 20th century when it was a significant issue in the campaigns of both Alfred E. Smith and John F. Kennedy. The Know Nothing Party utilized this widespread public sentiment to appeal to broad segments of the population, regardless of political persuasion – the party succeeded because they expressed a sizable quantum of views as a single issue of national concern: the immigrant problem. With a single and unified voice, the party was able to rally voters from all parts of the ideological spectrum. Curiously, the party's nativist myopia would mean both its success and its demise.

Dissatisfaction over the flood of immigrants led to tremendous, albeit initially muted dissatisfaction with the major political parties. While Morse and Beecher were leading pundits on the issue at the time, and the public imagination had been captured by "first-hand accounts" like Monk's, few individuals emerged to champion the Nativist cause, certainly not the prominent political parties of the day. The Democrats were perceived as relying too heavily on the immigrant vote; the Whigs too fragmented. The Republicans, who would gloriously and fatally usurp the Whigs from the political dais in 1860, would be too embroiled in the slavery controversy to offer anything.[22]   The only available solution was to form local parties – and, in time, to coordinate them.

In 1849, a group of working Protestants banded together to form a secret fraternal organization in New York to address the growing "immigrant problem." Known as the "Order of the Star-Spangled Banner," the group became the nucleus of the Know Nothing Party. Soon afterwards, similar lodges began crystallizing in every major American city. It was in these secretive clubs that members met to consult about political candidates, incumbents, and coordinate their voting patterns. Soon, the local offices began corresponding with nearby branches. Party officials from New York, Philadelphia and Boston toyed with the notion of going national, but for the moment focused their energies on gathering support locally. Whatever the case, it was clear that fifteen years after Morse first announced a Catholic conspiracy, the Know Nothing Party had finally arrived.

As late as 1850, the two-party system was, by all outward appearances, still healthy. Both the Democrats and Whigs were able to attract support in every section of the country and neither party was able to muster much more than 50 percent of the popular vote. The subsequent five years witnessed the complete disintegration of the two-party system in response to two key issues: foreign immigration and the expansion of slavery.

Around 1850, Know Nothing efforts turned towards electing only native-born, anti-immigration Americans to office. Members began agitating for a 21 year residence requirement for naturalization. As party membership and significance grew in the 1850s, the group slowly shed its clandestine character in hopes of becoming a serious national contender. As a national party, it officially called for severe restrictions on immigration, denying suffrage and public office to the foreign

---

[22] However, as president, Lincoln once sent a letter to his friend and confidant Joshua Speed in which he disavowed entirely the Known Nothing's nativism. In it he asks, "How can any one who abhors the oppression of negroes be in favor of degrading classes of white people?"

born, the ban of alcoholic beverages, and the daily reading of Protestant bibles in all public schools. By 1852 the Know Nothing Party was growing at a phenomenal rate. Though the 1852 elections won the party some notable gains, it would be another two years before the party seriously cut into the major political parties' – the Democrats and the Whigs – national power.

Growing rapidly, in 1854 the Know Nothings strategically allied themselves with the remaining splinter cell of Whigs who followed Millard Fillmore. Since more than 90 percent of Catholics in most cities voted Democratic, many Whig politicians decided to salvage the party by capitalizing on the Nativist threat. In the Know Nothing's very first national elections in 1854, the party sent forty representatives to Congress, practically swept the polls in Massachusetts, winning the governorship, every seat in the state senate, and all but two of the 378 seats in the state house of representatives. Know Nothing tickets were also victorious in state legislatures in Delaware, Rhode Island, New Hampshire, Connecticut, Maryland and, through the wise decision to join the remaining Whigs, also in Pennsylvania. The slow, prolonged disintegration of the Whig party was an immediate boon to the Know Nothings, as confused party-liners found themselves gravitating towards one of the few alternatives to the Democrats: the Know Nothings.

The 1854 elections proved so favorable – and so surprising – that the Know Nothings decided to roll out officially as a national political party, calling themselves, somewhat more euphemistically, the American Party. However impressive the party's quick gains, they should be attributed at least in part to major party decay and the divisive slavery issue, which had fragmented Democrats and was slowly giving rise to the Republican party. Additionally, the American Party's decision to stay neutral on slavery attracted voters committed to preserving the Union.

By 1855, just one year after the American Party scored its first coup in Massachusetts and Delaware, it captured control of all New England governorships and most legislatures except in Vermont and Maine. The American Party also became the dominant opposition party to the panicky Democrats in New York, Pennsylvania, Maryland, Virginia, Tennessee, Georgia, Alabama, Mississippi, and Louisiana. The South proved especially fertile for Know Nothing dominance, as the 1854 arrival of the Kansas-Nebraska Act had torn the Whig party apart. Southern Whigs generally supported the Act while Northern Whigs strongly opposed it. Many Southerners, sensing the power-splitting rift in the Whigs, were attracted to the Know-Nothing Party – after all, they appeared to stand for states' rights, anti-immigration, and stood neutral on slavery. In just five years, the Know Nothings had exhibited the political prowess of the established Democrats, becoming just as powerful as they deftly filled the vacuum created by the Whigs' demise. Nativism seemed on the verge of carrying the nation. The New York Herald despondently predicted that in 1856 a Know Nothing would be elected President. Several American Party leaders and sympathizers acknowledged that the party's victory in a national election was assured, and would likely result in violence, possibly revolution. Alas, the Know Nothings' rise would be as meteoric as their decline.

When Congress assembled in December, 1855, 43 representatives were avowed members of the Know Nothing Party, an additional 32 were reputed but undeclared supporters. In 1856, Horace Greeley opined that "the majority of the Banks men" – in reference to Nathaniel P. Banks, Speaker of the House of Representatives – "are now members of Know Nothing councils and some twenty or thirty of them actually believe in that swindle. Half of the Massachusetts delegation, two-thirds of that of Ohio and nearly all of that of Pennsylvania are Know Nothings." Publicly backing Millard Fillmore as a presidential candidate in 1856, the American Party won more than 21% of the popular vote and eight electoral votes. Though the stiff, unmarried Democratic candidate James Buchanan would take the Presidency, even more significant than the Know Nothing performance was the emergence of a new, sectional party composed of ex-Whigs, Free-Soil Democrats, and antislavery groups. The Republican Party, as it was called, opposed the extension of slavery and promised a free-labor society with expanded economic opportunities for all people, white or black. While Buchanan won with 174 electoral votes, the divided opposition captured more popular votes, the Republican party taking 1,335,264 votes (114 in the electoral college), and the American Party receiving 874,534 votes. The Republicans' powerful showing appeared an ill omen for Southerners, who walked away from the election with a hollow victory in the placatory and ineffectual Buchanan.

The year 1856 would mark both the peak and the beginning of the end of Know Nothing power. At the American Party convention in Philadelphia in 1857, the party split along sectional lines over the same issue that would throw the nation into civil war four years later. That so many were so united in denying Catholics and immigrants – in other words, predominantly whites – suffrage and citizenship, but drew the line on the question of slavery can only be regarded as a testament to the incredibly divisive forces that threatened to tear the Union apart. The violence and corruption that had come in the wake of the Kansas-Nebraska Act had infuriated anti-slavery Northerners, uprooted their faith in the old political system and past formulas of compromise. In what came to be known as "Bloody Kansas," in May of 1856, pro-slavery forces rode into Lawrence, Kansas, a Freesoil stronghold, and savagely burned the town to the ground. That same year, Representative Charles Sumner of Massachusetts received his fabled beating from South Carolina Congressman Preston Brooks.

"Bleeding Sumner" and "Bloody Kansas" became rallying cries in the North – calls that many within the Know Nothing Party felt duty and honor-bound to answer. The issue of slavery took center stage in American politics as battle lines were draw, both figuratively and, ultimately, literally. The Republican Party had firmly staked its ground as the abolitionist party and the Know Nothings had little room to insert itself on either side of the debate of the day, rendering itself and the issue of immigration a mere afterthought going into the election of 1860. The Republicans were invigorated, and appeared to possess a vim that made the still-young American Party seem irrelevant and decrepit by comparison. With the emergence of the Republican Party marking the path toward the restoration of a two-party system in America, the Know Nothings were largely absorbed along sectional, slavery-based lines and did not bother to nominate a candidate. Despite regular spasm of anti-immigrant and race-based political activism, nativism would never again rear its head in the form of an organized political party. Just as the Anti-Masons core doctrine was sidelined by distracting, external political struggles, so too did the Know Nothings miss their chance to capitalize on their early successes. The party was over.

(Don't) Raise a Glass to Liberty: The Prohibition Party

"Prohibition has made nothing but trouble."

— Al Capone

The term "Prohibition" typically conjures up cultural images of Hollywood's *The Untouchables*, famous underworld figures like Al Capone, and a string of archaic terms such as "speakeasy," "flapper" and "bootlegger." However, the story of prohibition in America spans a cultural and political history that predates the founding of the nation and continues to the present day. Most striking of all, perhaps, is the fact that the Prohibition Party has been, by nearly every measure, one of the most successful Doctrinal third parties in U.S. history, having attained, at least temporarily, its principal aim: the national prohibition of alcohol.

The Prohibition Party was formally formed in 1869 to provide a political voice to the socio-religious temperance and prohibition movements, and to this day the party remains the longest surviving third party in America. The party is best known for its role in the ratification of the Eighteenth Amendment to the Constitution and the passage of the Volstead Act, which gave rise to the eponymous age simply referred to as Prohibition. Paradoxically, though, the enactment of nation-wide prohibition removed the party's raison d'être and it eventually became a victim of its own success. Furthermore, the abrupt rise in violence during Prohibition refuted the claims made by prohibitionists that prohibition alone would solve America's social ills.

The drive to limit or prohibit the consumption of intoxicating beverages in the United States is not a modern phenomenon. Efforts at temperance and prohibition, calling for a temperate or responsible use of alcohol, or total abstinence from alcoholic beverages, existed in colonial America from its earliest days. In the 1630s, Massachusetts legislators enacted a rule that no person should remain in any inn or drinking establishment, "longer than necessary, upon payne [sic] of 20 Schillings for every offense." Brewers and distillers were taxed to gain revenue for the colonies, as well as to discourage the consumption of alcohol. In 1644, the New

York colony approved an excise tax on beer, wine, and brandy. In 1645, Massachusetts restricted drinkers by declaring more than half a pint at one time to be excessive, and "tippling, above ye space of half an hour" was forbidden. In 1733, the Georgia colony had the dubious distinction of being the first colony to establish a colony-wide prohibition edict. Despite efforts to enforce a dry colony, though, Georgia was thwarted by bootleggers from the Carolinas and the law was rescinded in 1742.

As with most of the farthest reaching social movements impacting American history, temperance and prohibition attracted the attention of the clergy. During the revolutionary period, most religious groups espoused a temperance stance within their congregations. Methodists and Presbyterians, however, asked for the total abstinence from alcohol of their members. John Wesley, an early Methodist leader, denounced distilling as a sin and called for its prohibition in 1773. On the heels of Wesley's appeal for prohibition came the publication of a pamphlet entitled "The Mighty Destroyer Displayed and Some Account of the Dreadful Havoc Made by the Mistaken Use, As Well As the Abuse, of Distilled Spiritous Liquors," by Anthony Benezet, a member of the Society of Friends and the founder of the world's first abolitionist society (of which Benjamin Franklin served as President). Benezet's essay advised against the use of any drink "which is liable to steal away a man's senses and render him foolish, irascible, uncontrollable, and dangerous." In time, the calls from the pulpit would reach the statehouse.

As the American Revolution approached, economic change and urbanization were accompanied by increasing poverty, unemployment, and crime. Such social problems were often blamed on drunkenness. The War for Independence, however, interrupted the drive for alcohol regulation as greater urgencies consumed the nation. Following the Revolutionary War, the metamorphosis of America accelerated; the new nation experienced radical social, political, and economic changes that affected every segment of society. Social control over alcohol abuse declined, anti-drunkenness ordinances were relaxed and alcohol-related problems increased dramatically. It was in this environment that people began seeking an explanation and a solution for drinking problems.

A suggestion came from one of the foremost physicians of the period, Dr. Benjamin Rush. In 1784, Dr. Rush argued that the excessive use of alcohol was injurious to physical and psychological health; nonetheless, Dr. Rush advocated for temperance rather than prohibition. Such advocacy helped spawn temperance and prohibitionist societies throughout the United States. In 1789, about 200 farmers in Litchfield, Connecticut began the first loose association of a temperance movement by prohibiting workers from drinking alcohol. Similar associations were formed in Virginia in 1800 and New York State in 1808. Within the next decade other temperance organizations were formed throughout the other states.

The American Temperance Society was founded in Boston in 1826 and benefited from the same religious and moral fervor that helped buoy the Anti-Masons of the time. Within 10 years the society claimed more than 8,000 local groups and over 1,500,000 members – that out of a population of less than 13 million individuals. Between 1830 and 1840, most temperance organizations began to argue that the only way to prevent drunkenness was to eliminate the consumption of alcohol outright; the Temperance Society became the Abstinence Society. The Independent Order of Good Templars, the Sons of Temperance, the Templars of Honor and Temperance, the Anti-Saloon League, and other groups were formed and grew rapidly. Thanks at least in part to the presence and activities of these societies, political action began to take place at the state and territory level.

In 1843 the Oregon Territory enacted the first prohibition law in the new nation, although it was repealed five years later. In 1846 Maine was the first state

74

to have a prohibition law, but this legislation, too, was defeated several times throughout the next decade. Towns and localities voted to become "dry," as did a dozen other states. In succeeding years, though, most of those laws were either voided by court action or repealed. The stresses and privations of the Civil War later wiped out most of the few remaining gains made by the temperance movement. With the conclusion of this conflict, however, the temperance and prohibition movements were free to reemerge with a vengeance.

Indeed, the movement was strongest in the swiftly opening west, where the male-dominated saloon societies of the cattle and gold-mining towns saw soaring rates of alcohol consumption; consequently, social and economic ills were most acute in these areas. Women, as the principal victims of alcohol-fueled domestic abuse and impoverishment, began to hold prayer vigils in the streets outside of the saloons in many of these towns. With the passage of time, the temperance societies became more and more extreme in their goals and actions.

Indeed, the movement even turned to violence to prevent the consumption of alcohol in America, and to draw attention to the cause. Eventually, one of America's more colorful figures emerged from the movement. Carrie Nation's calls to "smash, women, smash!," inspired axe-wielding prohibitionists to storm into saloons and reduce their bars, bottles, glasses, mirrors, tables and chairs to splinters and shards. Nation, a large woman (nearly 6 feet tall and 175 pounds), described herself as "a bulldog running along at the feet of Jesus, barking at what he doesn't like," and claimed a divine ordination to promote temperance by smashing up bars.

Although much publicity has focused on Carrie Nation and her Women's Christian Temperance Union as the catalyst for 20th century Prohibition, it was actually the Anti-Saloon League that led the way for a dry nation. Self-described as "[t]he church in action against the saloon," the League initially used church services to plead its case and recruited members - and donations - after services. Part of the success of the League was the nature of its organization: a loose confederation of evangelical churches that crossed denominational boundaries. Baptists, Methodists, and members of the Church of Christ, for example, worked together for the shared cause.

Following the standard trajectory of social and religious movements in American history, a national party was eventually formed to give political voice to the disparate organizations seeking the prohibition of alcohol. In 1869, The Prohibition Party was founded and held its first convention in Chicago, Illinois. The Prohibition Party ran its first presidential candidate in the 1872 election where James Black secured a disappointing 5,608 votes. Political success began to truly manifest itself toward the turn of the century. Prohibition Party presidential candidates polled over 100,000 votes at each election from 1884 to 1920. The Prohibition Party elected Kittel Halvorson of Minnesota to Congress in 1890, and in 1904 it elected 204 local officials in just one county, Venango County, in Pennsylvania. By 1916 the party elected Sidney Catts governor of Florida.

In 1906, the Anti-Saloon League, under the direction of Wayne B. Wheeler, led a spectacular fight against the reelection of Ohio Governor Myron T. Herrick. The defeat of the Herrick campaign was the first great political victory for the Anti-Saloon League and Prohibitionists. Wheeler became the attorney and general counsel for the national Anti-Saloon League, a member of the executive committee, and its head lobbyist. He became widely known as the "dry boss" because of his enormous influence and power. Justin Steuart, Wheeler's former Publicity Secretary, once remarked that

> Wayne B. Wheeler controlled six congresses, dictated to two presidents of the United States, directed legislation in most of the States of the Union, picked the candidates for the more important elective state and federal offices, held the balance of power in both Republican and Democratic parties, distributed

76

more patronage than any dozen other men, supervised a federal bureau from outside without official authority, and was recognized by friend and foe alike as the most masterful and powerful single individual in the United States.

The league was so powerful that even national politicians feared its strength.

The League considered itself "omnipartisan," working for bipartisan support of its cause. This "omnipartisanship" was novel for an emerging third party, and likely spared the Prohibition Party the fate of so many other third parties, namely the usurpation of their platform or absorption by a major party. By concentrating on candidates who were favorable to its objectives, regardless of political party, it held weight in many places and gradually increased its power in legislative bodies. The League retained attorneys to force closure of saloons, influenced the elections of officials whom it favored, and had its own periodical, *The American Issue*. This barrage of continuous information began to sway public opinion about saloons and about alcohol in general.

Business leaders began to see the benefits of the temperance movement. Besides any religious beliefs they may have harbored, their reasoning embraced the notion that sobriety would increase productivity. Supporters of the League included John D. Rockefeller Sr., Henry Ford, Pierre DuPont, and the Pillsbury family. Future President Herbert Hoover was a strong supporter of the temperance movement. It was through the business community that the League acquired the majority of its donations to fight the saloon. At the height of the movement, between 1910 and 1923, the League collected up to $2 million a year in revenue in support of its agenda.

The Prohibition Party, its candidates, and the organizations supporting its goals had a significant impact, affecting legislation at the local level almost immediately. By 1905, three American states had already outlawed alcohol; by 1912 it was up to nine states; and, by 1916, legal prohibition was already in effect in more than half the states in the union. Alcohol remained available in these "dry" states, however, thanks to a loophole in the legal framework of prohibition - the postal service. Because the postal service was run by the federal government instead of the state governments, liquor could be mail ordered from a wet state. This infuriated the "dries" and in 1913, the Interstate Liquor Act was passed. This act made it illegal to send liquor to a dry state. Following on the heels of this success, prohibitionists launched a national drive for a constitutional amendment prohibiting the manufacture and sale of alcoholic beverages. This effort, however, initially failed to garner the necessary support in the House of Representatives. Despite that national failure, state legislatures increasingly came under the control of prohibition supporters.

During World War I, prohibition advocates and politicians buttressed their cause through the 1917 Food and Fuel Control Act, which contained a section prohibiting the manufacture of distilled liquor, beer, and wine. Support was given to this measure by non-prohibitionists who were convinced that grain production should be devoted to food, not drink, during wartime. Moreover, an amendment to existing legislation made it unlawful to use the mail to send liquor advertisements to persons in dry territory. This steady drumbeat of legislation was all aimed, though, at a single objective: outright national prohibition. In December 1917, Congress began the Constitutional amendment process by passing a resolution that would make the entire country dry. Many states did not wait for ratification and 31 promptly adopted statewide laws supporting prohibition.

On January 16, 1919 the 18th Amendment was ratified. All hard liquor with over 40% alcohol content (80 proof) was banned. The 18th Amendment explicitly banned the "manufacture, sale, or transportation of intoxicating liquors ... for beverage purposes." The amendment was able to pass, in some considerable part, as a result of support from many non-prohibitionists who believed the amendment only banned hard liquors.   Yet before the Amendment took effect on January 16, 1920, in October of 1919, the Volstead Act was passed, which extended the ban to all alcohol having over *0.5%* alcohol content. The act effectively banned all forms of alcoholic beverages, with the exception of some non-alcoholic beers.   The Prohibition Era had begun.

National prohibition was viewed as a panacea. Prohibition was meant to eliminate the consumption of alcohol, and thereby reduce crime, poverty and the rest of society's ills, whilst improving the economy and wellbeing of the nation. At the dawn of Prohibition, Reverend Billy Sunday proclaimed that "[t]he reign of tears is over. The slums will soon be a memory. We will turn our prisons into factories and our jails into storehouses and corncribs. Men will walk upright now, women will smile and children will laugh. Hell will be forever for rent." Despite the great intentions and utopic hope, Prohibition proved an abject failure, ironically giving rise to increased crime, incarceration, and leaving the U.S. with a legacy of organized crime that persists to this day.

During Prohibition none of the socio-economic benefits came to fruition. Arrests for drunkenness, disorderly conduct, and drunk driving, the federal prison population, and a host of other indicators of societal ills increased at alarming rates. Bootlegging became widespread and a staple of organized crime.   Home stills sprouted up in isolated places as well as bathtubs on Park Avenue. Illegal drinking establishments, or speakeasies, sprang up throughout the country.   Concealment of alcohol on one's person became an art form, and the flask a fashion accessory. Everything from hollow canes to hollow books were used to hide spirits. Enforcement of prohibition was an extremely difficult, costly and often violent proposition for law enforcement at all levels.   Organized crime during Prohibition had such a profound impact on the American psyche and society that Al Capone's conviction captured the headline of the Chicago Sunday Tribune, despite occurring on the same day as the death of America's most prolific and celebrated inventor, Thomas Edison.

The successes of the Prohibition Party quickly unraveled. In 1932, both the Republican and Democratic Party platforms called for the repeal of prohibition. Congress passed a resolution proposing repeal in 1933 and it was promptly ratified by three-fourths of the states before year's end. Having engaged in omnipartisanship, essentially being both a political party within the system as well as a social movement endorsing candidates from opposition parties that embraced their doctrinal ideology, the Prohibition Party was poorly positioned to resist when the political winds shifted and the major parties abandoned the prohibition cause. The 21st Amendment remains the only amendment repealing a previously adopted one. Today the Prohibition Party persists but is plagued by public indifference to the cause and internecine fighting, which caused a split in the party in 2003. Presidential candidates have failed to capture a significant segment of the popular vote since the end of Prohibition.

Despite the failures of Prohibition, the Prohibition Party, and more specifically the theories behind prohibition of any kind, continue to impact the nation. The culture wars of the 1960s and the perceived breakdown of social mores inspired a legal assault on psychotropic substances of all kinds. Like the arguments made in favor of the prohibition of alcohol, advocates of drug prohibition have claimed that prohibition is the exclusive means to eliminate use of drugs and their associated vice. Opponents of drug prohibition and America's "War on Drugs" point to the rise of narco-traffickers and drug-fueled gang violence as a predictable consequence of such measures. Today's pro-prohibition forces, and the Prohibition Party, persist, despite all evidence of their failure to achieve their stated aim – social welfare.

The Prohibition Party's legacy in the pantheon of American third parties, however, is still very much relevant. The mere example of even temporary success for a third party surely inspires hope amongst aspiring third parties, whether Doctrinal or Realignment in nature. Ironically, it may be that current movements and parties advocating for the decriminalization and legalization of marijuana for medical and recreational purposes see the incrementalism of the Prohibition Party as a blue print for their own success. State-by-state recreational decriminalization and legal medical marijuana is spreading across the nation much as prohibition once did. Even the federal government has curtailed its enforcement of federal law and made exceptions to strict policies regarding health care coverage for veterans living in states where medical marijuana is legal. It could be just a matter of time before, yet again, a major party adopts this doctrinal position as its own in a continuance of the long story of third parties in America.

Parties of The People:
Greenback & Populist Parties

*We cordially invite all patriotic and free citizens ... to abandon all old parties and
unite with us in establishing a new party of the people ...*

- Greenback Party Platform

America's centennial election was one of the most disputed in U.S. history. Modern observers will see countless parallels between 1876 and the contentious 2000 presidential elections. Like the 2000 election, the 1876 vote came down to a question of disputed electoral votes, and the candidate who won the popular vote did not become president. In 1876 the president-elect was even decided by a quasi-judicial body. Yet despite the acrimony of the election, the two major party candidates embraced similar positions on the major issues of the day, especially on the question of hard currency. In a still largely rural and agrarian America, the shift away from paper money was strongly opposed by farmers, opening the way to a third party to take advantage of this issue.

The Greenback Party, so named after the nickname for America's paper money, was formed to fill this political void; its successor party, the Populists, broadened their appeal by adding urban labor to its agricultural base. For a time it appeared as though the Populists would cause a realignment in American politics and achieve major party status. Ultimately, both parties were essentially doctrinal in nature and suffered the typical fate of doctrinal third parties. Greenback and Populist ideas eventually come to fruition, though enacted by the Democratic and Republican Parties.

During the American Civil War, National Banking Acts were adopted to help fund the Union war effort. In practice, this allowed the government to simply print money as it was needed, greatly increasing inflation and devaluing America's currency. Following a series of economic crises after the Civil War, which culminated in the Panic of 1873, the country was put back on the gold standard. The resulting tightening of the nation's money supply hit debtors, especially farmers, particularly hard.

Immediately after the Civil War, the Democratic Party seemed to be on the verge of embracing soft money in an attempt to broaden their appeal beyond the South. The 1868 party platform contained a greenback plank to pay off Civil War debts with paper currency rather than in gold specie. However, the nomination of New York governor Horatio Seymour, a hard money advocate who distanced himself as much as possible from this position, ended this prospect. With the Republican and Democratic Parties firmly behind hard money, Greenbackers needed a party of their own.

Launched at a meeting in 1874, the Greenback Party nominated industrialist and philanthropist Peter Cooper to run for president in 1876 as their first presidential candidate. As his running mate the Greenback Party selected Samuel Fenton Cary. Cary had succeeded Rutherford B. Hayes, the eventual winner of the 1876 contest, in Ohio's 2nd congressional district when Hayes became Governor of Ohio. In addition to soft money, the Greenback Party sought the restoration of bimetallism – the fixed exchange of paper curency for gold or silver, which had been effectively abandoned following the Panic of 1873.

The combination of soft money and a gold-silver system of bimetallism had widespread support in the United States. Newly discovered silver deposits in western states, such as the Comstock Lode, flooded the market with the precious metal. Fixing the price of silver through bimetallism, thus avoiding a collapse in the price as supply surged, was supported by the farmers who saw bimetallism as a way to spur inflation, allowing the price of their crops to rise and help them pay off their onerous debts. Silver miners and mining interests supported bimetallism for essentially the same economic reasons, namely fixing the price of silver above its natural price as dictated by the laws of supply and demand. When the Coinage Act of 1873 demonetized silver, the money supply tightened, the price of silver plummeted and deflation occurred. The Coinage Act was referred to by supporters of silver and bimetallism as The Crime of '73. Silver and soft money loomed large on the campaign trail as the 1876 election approached and would continue to be a central issue in the national debate for years to come.

Cooper drew less than one percent of the popular vote in 1876. Cooper's poor showing and the seeming consensus of the major parties on the issue of hard money did not prevent some success for the advocates of bimetallism and soft money. In 1878 the Bland-Allison Act was passed over the veto of President Hayes. The Act's central aim was to subsidize the silver mining interests in the mountain states and inflate prices. Though silver was to be purchased at market prices, the government would resume minting silver coins at a ratio of 16:1; in other words, 16 troy ounces of silver would be equivalent to a single ounce of gold regardless of the metals' respective market values. The Hayes Administration, however, eviscerated the law's intent by purchasing only the minimum quantity of silver required by the Bland-Allison Act. The U.S. remained on a gold-standard.

The money issue remained alive and well in the mid-term elections of 1878. That year Greenback candidates polled well and captured more than one million votes, resulting in 13 seats in the 46th Congress. Amongst this first class of successful Greenback Party candidates was James B. Weaver, a Civil War veteran who rose from the rank of Private to Colonel during that conflict and was even elevated temporarily to the rank of Brigadier General. Weaver became the Greenback Party's candidate for president in 1880.

For the 1880 election the Greenback Party expanded its platform beyond its doctrinal motivation of soft money. The Greenback Party platform voiced support for a graduated income tax, an eight hour workday and women's suffrage. The Greenback Party also gave political voice to the demand for health and safety protections for labor, including the curtailment of child labor. Finally, the Greenbackers called for greater regulation of interstate commerce as a way to blunt the power of the railroads and other industrial interests.

These seemingly radical positions became cornerstones of the Progressive Era of American politics, and now seem quite commonplace in America. During this period the Greenback's successor party, the Populist Party, as well as the Prohibition Party and the Progressive wing of the Republican Party that eventually went on to form the Bull Moose Party under Theodore Roosevelt, all advocated these and many other progressive policies. These policies all ultimately found fertile ground in the politics and policies of the American government, though under Republican and Democratic, rather than third party, administrations.

In the 1880 election Weaver received over 300,000 votes, or approximately three percent of the total. Weaver's vote total overwhelmingly exceeded the popular vote difference between Republican James Garfield and his main rival, Democrat Winfield Hancock. The 1880 vote remains the closest election in U.S. history with Garfield winning 4,446,158 votes to Hancock's 4,444,260. Weaver's candidacy essentially tipped the election to Garfield; the Greenback Party drew much of its support from disaffected Democrats and Weaver held the balance in Indiana, which went for Garfield.[23]

As victory in this single state would have handed the presidency to Hancock, the Greenback Party essentially thwarted a potential realignment away from postbellum Republican Party dominance. Nonetheless, the Democrats did manage to briefly capture the White House four years later. Proof of the Greenback appeal to Democrats and its potential to affect the outcome of elections came swiftly after the 1880 election. In 1882 the Greenback party cross-endorsed with Democratic Party candidates, electing Democrat Ben Butler as governor of the Republican stronghold of Massachusetts. Greenback-Democratic fusion tickets also won the governorships in Michigan and Maine. However, these fusion victories

---

[23] The parallels between this election and the dynamic that played out in 2000 are too obvious to mention.

would prove pyrrhic. Cross-party endorsement by the Greenback Party prevented the party from emerging as a true alternative to the major parties.

Cross-endorsement with Democrats was not the only undoing of the Greenback Party. In a staggering display of political bipolar disorder the Greenback Party allied itself with Republicans in the South to draw upon the agrarian, and newly enfranchised African American electorate. Simultaneously, following their successes in Maine, Massachusetts and Michigan, the Greenback Party was more likely to join Democrats in the North who possessed elements more sympathetic to their soft money position. The Greenbacks never found their political footing as a national party. Butler's 1884 presidential candidacy as a Greenback polled little more than half of Weaver's 1880 total. Economic recovery after the Panic of 1873 proved fatal to the Greenback Party, and thereafter the party ceased to exist.

The end of the Greenback Party did not mark the end of the money issue in American politics. Nor did it end the discontent felt by many rural and western interests that the Democratic and Republican Parties were beholden to the money-interests of east coast bankers and industrialists. When economic hardship again struck the nation in the late 1880s, a group of farmers joined with labor to revive the populist and progressive message of the Greenback Party. By 1892 the People's Party, known as the Populists, emerged as the Greenbacks reincarnate, only this time with a broader agenda and a broader electorate.

At the same time that the Greenback Party was fielding Peter Cooper for president in 1876, groups of farmers were banding together to blunt the effects of depreciation and their worsening economic circumstances. These Farmers' Alliances set up cooperative stores and established their own mills to maintain greater control over the costs of farming. However, resistance by commodities brokers and other monied interests proved too much for the loose-knit network of Farmers' Alliances as a purely economic movement. As the economy worsened again, the

Farmers' Alliances joined forces with other currency reformers and with urban labor, through the Knights of Labor, to launch a new party.

The Populist Party was born in the midst of America's Gilded Age, a time of increased wealth disparity. America remained on the gold standard and the major parties remained firmly in the pro-gold camp. The decades-long struggle for the free coinage of silver and soft money policies was going nowhere. In 1890, The Sherman Silver Purchase Act was enacted into law. The Act, however, did nothing to promote soft money or silver coinage. The Act did increase the required annual purchase of silver by the Federal government from the $2-4 million required under the Bland-Allison Act (of which only the minimum was ever procured) by requiring the U.S. to purchase an additional 4.5 million ounces of silver bullion every month. Though a seeming victory for silver interests the effect was that speculators abused a loophole: the silver was to be purchased with notes redeemable for either silver or gold. These speculators redeemed the notes for gold, utterly depleting the nation's gold supply in the process and sparking an economic crisis a few years later.

With mere lip-service being paid to the advocates for free silver and soft money, the forces of labor and agriculture met in Omaha, Nebraska in 1892 to launch their new party. In their 1892 convention the Populists seemed to simply pick up where the Greenback Party had left off at its peak. The party platform adopted in Omaha called for a graduated income tax, an eight-hour workday, and government control of interstate commerce such as railroads, telegraphs and the newly emerging telephone. Of course the platform also called for the free coinage of silver. The party even nominated James B. Weaver as its candidate. The Populists also introduced a novel element to their platform – the direct elections of senators.

From the moment of its arrival it appeared the Populist Party would do what the Greenbacks had failed to do, achieve major party status. Weaver captured over one million votes and won the popular votes in Colorado, Kansas, Idaho, Nevada and North Dakota. Weaver split the electoral vote in North Dakota, which allowed their electoral votes to be allocated by congressional districts at the time, much as Maine and Nebraska do today. By this same system Weaver also picked up an electoral vote from Oregon where he came in second, bringing his electoral vote tally to 22. Populists also did well in congressional races, electing two Senators and eight members of the House of Representatives to the 52nd Congress. Populist congressional electoral success, and that of some allies in the Silver Party of Nevada and a Republican splinter group calling themselves Silver Republicans, helped to grow the bimetallist faction in the Congress over subsequent years.

During its life, the Populist Party embarked on some fantastic socio-political experimentation. The Populists were the first significant American political party to actively include women in the affairs of the party. Moreover, at a time when poisonous racial prejudice permeated all corners of American life, even some Southern Populists called for the end of racial divisions between poor blacks and poor whites. The gender and racial rapprochement of the Populists, however, did not mean the party was all-inclusive. Populists espoused strong nativist sentiments, and even had taken on strong tones of religious bigotry. Immigrants and Catholics, as well as Jews seen as part of the American and international banking establishment, were targeted as the cause of the nation's economic woes. Even the talk of racial conciliation went by the wayside when it was no longer politically expedient or necessary. The Populists had done well in prior elections and now possessed a clear political identity. The dream of a third party political breakthrough seemed within grasp.

Going into the 1896 election the Populists were riding a high wave of enthusiasm and success; however the meteoric rise of the Populists was about to come to an end. Even as the nation was turning toward silver as a way to fix the

89

nation's economic woes and rising nativist sentiments were stirring the white, protestant agrarian electorate to political action, the Populists were confronted by that perennial threat to all third parties - usurpation. The Populists were to be victims of their own success.

By 1896, the Democratic Party took up many of the Populist Party's causes at the national level. The Democrats nominated William Jennings Bryan, a fierce silverite and one of the nation's foremost political orators. The Populists were forced to choose between splitting the silver vote and handing the election to the Republican Party or nominate Bryan and risk being absorbed into the newly populist Democratic Party. The Populists opted for nominating Bryan. However, the Populists could not bring themselves to also nominate Bryan's conservative eastern running mate, Arthur Sewall. Though no agreement was made regarding whom would serve as vice president should Bryan win, the Populists nominated Georgian congressman Thomas E. Watson for vice president. The Populists hoped the split ticket would help preserve their political identity. Such hopes were futile and the Populists were at this point merely delaying the inevitable.

Bryan backed the Populist Party's opposition to the gold standard in his famous "Cross of Gold" speech. Bryan delivered the speech at the 1896 Democratic National Convention in Chicago using powerful religious imagery to make his point, and concluded by saying,

> Having behind us the producing masses of this nation and the world, supported by the commercial interests, the laboring interests and the toilers everywhere, we will answer their demand for a gold standard by saying to them, 'You shall not press down upon the brow of labor this crown of thorns, you shall not crucify mankind upon a cross of gold.

Through this speech Bryan firmly entrenched the Democratic Party in the bimetallism camp and secured his place as the leading national advocate for economic populism.

Bryan's campaign took him across the country on a national speaking tour. This strategy was a novelty for a presidential candidate. Prior to 1896 it was considered undignified for candidates to campaign actively; candidates left campaigning to their respective parties and traveled only sparingly to give a few speeches during the campaign. Bryan, however, went directly to the voters, using his powerful oratory to impress those who flocked to see him speak. In 100 days of campaigning, Bryan gave over 500 speeches to millions of voters. Though aided by modern modes of transportation, it was still a remarkable feat.

While Bryan saw his national stature rise during and after the 1896 election (he would run again as the Democratic nominee for President in 1900 and 1908), the fusion ticket formed between the Democrats and the Populists proved ruinous for the Populists and was ultimately unable to deliver the White House to Bryant. Alliance with the Democratic Party alienated the Populist's Republican allies in the South who viewed the Democratic Party as the bastion of white supremacist politics. This breach with southern Republicans opened the way for the absorption of Populists into the ranks of the Democratic Party. Though they attempted to regain their status as a separate party in the minds of voters, the damage had been done. After 1896 the Populist Party essentially ceased to exist.[24]

---

[24] Bryan and the Populists would long outlive the 1896 election in a rather surprising way, popular literature. Many have seen in L. Frank Baum's *Wizard of Oz* an allegory to the socio-economic conditions of the time, the populist movement, and even Bryan himself. It has been suggested that the scarecrow represents the American farmer, while the Tin Man personifies the urban industrial laborer. Bryan, known for his oratory (the lion's roar) but dismissed as having little substance behind his words, is represented by the Cowardly Lion. Dorothy fills the role of the lost "everyman" or ordinary individual in society.

The group travels down the yellow brick road – the gold standard – to the Emerald City, possibly the greenback currency linked to gold. The Wicked Witches of the East and West are seen to

Bryan lost the 1896 election by close to 600,000 votes. Running with his Democratic vice presidential candidate, Bryan captured over five times as many electoral votes as he did running with the Populist Watson. By the 1900 presidential campaign, the Populists saw their share of congressional seats shrinking. Many Populist voters supported Bryan and the Democratic Party again that year even though the Populists nominated a separate ticket. Though the Populists nominated a ticket in 1900, 1904, and 1908, the party had essentially been overwhelmed by Bryan and the Democratic shift to silver and other populist positions.

The socio-economic populism of the late 1800s perfectly illustrates the difficulties faced by third parties. Regardless of their appeal, the first-past-the-post system of American politics makes success by nascent political parties difficult to accomplish. Though the issue of soft money and bimetallism was initially rejected by the Democratic and Republican Parties, it eventually provided the Democratic Party with an issue from which they could break out of their post-bellum banishment and isolation in the former confederacy. Whether the Democratic Party adopted populism or the Populists captured the Democratic Party is hard to say, but the result was the same.

Though they went the way of nearly all third parties to date, the Populists and Greenbacks can lay claim to many long-term political, if not electoral, successes. While the Greenback Party began as a strictly Doctrinal party, its broadened platform and anti-realignment role in the 1880 election makes that label difficult to apply. Moreover, the latter manifestation of the movement under the Populist

---

exemplify the coastal business, banking, and industrial elites oppressing the Munchkins, the masses, who the wicked Witches keep, in the words of Baum, "in bondage for many years, making them work for her night and day." Even the famous twister can be seen as a metaphor for the economic turmoil roiling the nation.

Party label was, though still born of a desire to see soft money bimetallism prevail, even harder to categorize. The Populist Party is best understood as a broad-based doctrinal party with realignment properties.

By the time of the Populist Party's formation the populist movement had grown beyond the initial calls for soft money and free silver. Many of the positions endorsed by the Populists were shared by other third parties of the time, but were anathema to the entrenched powers of the major parties. This novelty and radicalism is the hallmark of a doctrinal party. Their later enactment into law or through constitutional amendments, after being appropriated by one major party or the other, is the very embodiment of realignment politics.

While the United States would remain on the gold standard until 1971, many other issues advocated by these two third parties came to fruition in the first two decades of the 20th century. The 16th Amendment to the U.S. constitution allowed for an income tax, and the 17th amendment shifted the election of senators from state legislatures to the people they represent. Women got the right to vote nationwide after the ratification of the 19th Amendment. Not since the 13th, 14th and 15th Amendments passed in quick succession after the Civil War had so many changes to the U.S. constitution been made so rapidly. Earlier in the century labor and economic reforms improved the lives of workers in the ways envisioned by the Greenback, Populist and other third parties in the late 19th century. The momentum for these changes is the result of third party action.

Voters of The World Unite:
The Socialist Party

I would not lead you into the Promised Land if I could, because if I led you in, someone else would lead you out.

- Eugene V. Debs

"Socialism" has long been amongst the dirtiest words in the American political lexicon. Nonetheless, this movement in all its stripes has found fertile ground in America's political landscape for over a century. Founded from an amalgam of disparate left-leaning labor and political groups in 1901, the Socialist Party eventually disintegrated into its former constituent parts and ideologies. Prior to this break-down, however, the Socialist Party enjoyed significant electoral success at the state and national level and played an influential role in molding the national dialogue during some of its greatest trials and tribulations: The Great Depression, World War II, and The Cold War. While maintaining its doctrinal core, and in many respects suffering from it, the Socialist Party helped to realign and reform America through the adoption by Franklin Roosevelt, in the form of the New Deal, of many of the party's platform policies.

Despite the advent of political populism at the close of the 19th century, the social upheaval wrought by the rapid industrialization and urbanization of the nation could not be sated by any one movement or any one ideology. Populism had found fertile ground in the agricultural regions of the nation, primarily in the west and mid-west; on the east coast and in urban centers, however, labor organizations, motivated by socialist political theory, were drawing supporters and embarking on political activism through protest and campaigning. By the 1900 presidential election, two socialist groups, the Social Democratic Party and the Socialist Labor Party, joined forces to endorse the candidacy of Eugene V. Debs; Debs would run for president under the Socialist banner five times throughout his life. In 1901, the Social Democratic Party absorbed portions of the Socialist Labor Party that had seceded and formed the Socialist Party of America. Though many labor leaders and socialists played important roles in the history of socialism and the Socialist Party in the United States, without Debs there was no party.

Debs was foreordained for subversion. Debs's parents fled France to realize their forbidden love; his father, Jean Daniel, came from a prosperous Protestant family while his mother, Mary Marguerite Bettrich, hailed from Roman Catholic working-class stock. Despite coming from a long line of merchants and bankers, Debs's father pursued art and literature, and he named his first-born son after his literary heroes, Eugène Sue and Victor Hugo. Sunday evenings in the Debs household were spent with readings from Goethe, Dumas, and Rousseau, in addition to Sue and Hugo, as well as others amongst the Romantics. Debs learned French and German in this way, and would frequently reread Hugo's *Les Miserables* throughout his life. Although Debs was an avid reader and did well in school, he terminated his formal education at the age of fourteen, against the protests of his parents, to work. Eventually he took a job at the railroad that would change his life forever.

Debs, ever likeable and industrious, was quickly promoted to railroad fireman. Following a friend's fatal slip and fall under a train Debs left railroading to become a billing clerk at a wholesale grocery company, but he never ceased to feel a kinship with the railroad workers. In February 1877, he attended the founding meeting of the Brotherhood of Locomotive Firemen and was elected recording secretary. The next year he ran as a Democrat and was elected city clerk in his hometown of Terre Haute, Indiana and reelected the following year. Soon Debs was made secretary-treasurer of the Brotherhood and editor of its journal; under Debs's leadership, membership in the Brotherhood grew from little over 1,000 to nearly 5,000 within a few years. In 1884, Debs was elected to a single term in the Indiana state legislature. Debs the labor and political leader had arrived.

In 1893, Debs formed the American Railway Union. The ARU allowed for membership of all railway employees, not just those trained in skilled crafts as the American Federation of Labor insisted upon at the time. The next year, the great

Pullman Strike was a critical event in the history of labor in America, and in the life of Debs. In spite of Debs's warnings against a strike, the ARU membership refused to handle Pullman cars or any other railroad car attached to them, including those carrying U.S. Mail. The U.S. Army was sent in to restore the delivery of mail – the ensuing violence destroyed an estimated $80 million worth of property, and despite his opposition to the strike Debs was sent to jail for interfering with the mail.

In prison Debs read the works of Karl Marx, and upon his release embarked on his socialist political career. Debs began a national lecture tour. Speaking with fiery oration to overflowing crowds, Debs's speeches became ever more radical, and his popularity grew. Years later at Deb's eulogy the journalist and former Socialist candidate for Congress, Heywood Broun, described Debs with a quote from a skeptic he had interviewed at a Debs rally: "That old man with the burning eyes actually believes that there can be such a thing as the brotherhood of man. And that's not the funniest part of it. As long as he's around I believe it myself." In hindsight, given his outsized role in the socialist movement, however, Debs's eulogy could easily have been the party's.

With the looming election of 1896 there was talk of running Debs as the Populist Party candidate, but the maneuvering of William Jennings Bryan to fuse Populism with the Democratic Party quickly quashed that idea. Debs supported Bryan in the election, but with Bryan's defeat to William McKinley, Debs came to see the two major parties as irredeemably beholden to capitalist corporations. Debs publicly declared himself a Socialist, pronouncing that "[t]he issue is Socialism versus Capitalism. I am for Socialism because I am for humanity."

Debs's Socialism was uniquely American. Despite the atheism most commonly associated with Marxist theory, Debs proclaimed that Socialism was "[m]erely Christianity in action." Debs became a Christ-like figure in the Socialist movement. He was viewed as having undergone a born-again conversion to

Socialism while imprisoned and, having first refused the nomination to run for president, was viewed as a martyr by those who rejoiced in his reversal following pleadings by party leaders to take up the mantle. Debs was also the only figure that could heal the factionalism running rife within socialist America.

Socialism in America can be dated to Karl Marx's historic First International in 1864. The gathering of left-wing political groups and trade union organizations drew some support from American labor. America's first national labor union, dubbed appropriately the National Labor Union, sent a delegation to the Basel Congress of the First International in 1869. Though the National Labor Union hoped to enter politics as a third party, and despite Marx's move to relocate the International's headquarters to New York City, the movement dissolved by 1873. America would have to await a wholesale reorganization of its adherents to leftist politics to have a true socialist political party.

Socialist congresses were held in New York City in 1872, and again in Philadelphia in 1874. During the 1874 meeting the Social Democratic Workingmen's Party, America's first Marxist political movement, was formed. The Social Democratic Workingmen's Party barely survived this congress due to the lack of internal cohesion and organization. American socialists gathered again in Philadelphia in 1876 to disband the First International. Four days later these same groups held a Unity Congress to found the Workingmen's Party of the United States. This party would eventually be recast as the Socialist Labor Party two years later.

Since its founding, the Socialist Labor Party trended toward a more nationalist version of socialism that better fit the geographically separate and politically isolationist United States. In 1890, the aggressive and domineering Daniel De Leon, a lecturer of Latin American diplomacy at Columbia University, joined the party and quickly rose to become its national spokesperson and editor of its in-house publication, *The People.* Thereafter the party and the man became indistinguishable. The single-minded and doctrinal focus of De Leon bred factionalism as he rejected those who supported incrementalism or any notion of labor justice within a capitalist framework. In 1899, moderate socialists, under the leadership of figures such as Victor Berger, Morris Hillquit, and Debs, seceded from De Leon's group and splintered socialist America into the Social Labor Party and the Social Democratic Party, which proved more flexible and inclusive than the Social Labor Party. This division was to be short lived, however. By the next year Debs was able to bring together the Social Democratic Party and the Socialist Labor Party for a national campaign. Supported by both parties, Debs ran for president in 1900 and drew 87,945 voters to the socialist cause.

In 1901, Berger, Hillquist and Debs officially launched the Socialist Party of America. De Leon remained apart and his strident militancy repulsed potential followers of his quickly foundering movement. The Socialist Labor Party swiftly declined in stature while the Socialist Party, under the leadership of its founders and identified increasingly with the persona of Debs, flourished. In the 1904 presidential election, under the newly formed and relatively unified banner of the Socialist Party of America, Debs more than quadrupled, to 402,810 votes, his vote tally of four years earlier. During the 1908 election Debs rode throughout the United States on his campaign train, dubbed the *Red Special.* He was met by jubilant crowds and received near adoration in the press, even being compared to Abraham Lincoln. Nonetheless, due to economic prosperity and the populist split caused by Bryan's repeat candidacy, the 1908 vote was a disappointing 420,973, barely a blip above Debs's previous campaign.

After an unsuccessful run for Congress in 1904, Victor Berger won election in Wisconsin's 5th congressional district in 1910 becoming the first Socialist to serve in the United States Congress. Berger would fail at successive bids for

Congress only to return in 1918 after a stint in prison for speaking out against America's involvement in World War I. During his first term in Congress, Berger introduced the first bill of its kind to establish an old-age pension in the United States. When Berger returned to Washington to claim his seat the second time, Congress formed a special committee to determine whether a convicted felon and war opponent should be seated as a member of Congress; they concluded that he should not, and declared the seat vacant. Wisconsin promptly held a special election to fill the vacant seat, and elected Berger a second time. The House again refused to seat Berger, and the seat remained vacant until 1921, when Republican William H. Stafford claimed the seat after defeating Berger in the 1920 general election. Berger defeated Stafford in 1922 and was reelected in 1924 and 1926. Berger was allowed to serve these final terms without interference from Congress.

Along with Berger's terms in Congress, Meyer London of New York City was elected thrice to the House of Representatives, 1915-1919 and 1921-1923, respectively. The Socialist Party also enjoyed success in various mayoralties. Milwaukee, Wisconsin had an almost uninterrupted string of Socialist Mayors from 1910 to 1960. Reading, Pennsylvania was led by Socialist mayor J. Henry Stump from 1927-1931, 1935-1939, and again from 1943-1947. Bridgeport, Connecticut, Berkeley, California and Schenectady, New York also saw Socialist leadership during the first half of the 20th Century.

In time the Socialist Party ceased to emphasize the traditional Marxist struggle between "bourgeois" and "proletarians." Instead, the party spoke in an American vernacular of "capitalists" and "wage-earners" in its platform. In the coming years the party began using language long-identified with the Populists, marking an interesting convergence in third party history - here the realignment was triangulated; while the Democratic Party adopted elements of populism in 1894 with the cross-endorsements of William Jennings Bryan, so too did the Socialists twelve years later when the Democrats once again moved away from these positions. However, rather than the evolutionary process whereby third parties have shared their ideological elements with successor parties, such as the Liberty and Free Soil parties, the Socialists were not a true successor party to the Populists. Even so, the parties found themselves with common ground in the struggle against the socio-economic *status quo.*

Leading up to the next presidential campaign, the Socialist Party was increasingly viewed as a viable alternative to the Democratic and Republican parties. By the end of 1911, Socialists could count hundreds of elected officials amongst their ranks, including mayors and city councilmen, as well as Victor Berger in the House of Representatives. The party also enjoyed high readership of its 5 English-language dailies and over 250 English-language weeklies; the party also produced a number of foreign-language publications in the ethnic, working-class enclaves from which they drew great support.

The presidential election of 1912 proved to be the Socialist Party's most successful, and one of the most exciting in U.S. history. In that year, three major candidates faced off, including two men from the same party who had previously won the presidency! The Republican and Democratic parties were riven by division; Wilson would only be selected on the 46th ballot, and the Republicans were so divided that after ex-president Theodore Roosevelt swept the primary elections against incumbent William H. Taft, the party bosses engineered a reversal of the popular will, seating delegates for Taft in states Roosevelt had won, such as California. Unable to tolerate the machinations of party insiders, Roosevelt led his supporters out of the convention hall to begin an entirely new party.

The Socialist Party convention was not without its drama as well. Socialist politics in the United States have always suffered from divisions between revolutionaries and moderates. Seeking to build upon the recent successes of the

101

party, Berger and Hillquist conspired to remove the leading radical, Bill Haywood, a staunch advocate of the "overthrow of the capitalist system by forcible means if necessary," from the Socialist Party's National Executive Committee. Vitriolic accusations flew back-and-forth between the wings of the party, with Berger and Hillquist accusing Haywood of advocating murder and theft to attain his objectives. Eventually the party adopted a motion banning "any member who opposes political action or advocates crime, sabotage or other methods of violence as a weapon of the working class." Eventually this motion was used to oust Haywood from the party.

The absence of Debs, who remained in Terre Haute during the convention, guaranteed that Berger and Hillquist controlled the nominating process. Each man wanted to prevent Debs from running again and, unable to unite behind a single candidate, both supported their own candidates. However, Debs's name was offered and he secured the nomination on the first ballot. Nevertheless, party unity was rapidly restored when Berger's candidate, Emil Seidel, a former mayor of Milwaukee, was selected to run as Vice President; Hillquist's candidate was drafted as the campaign manager.

The party platform adopted at the convention was a fabulous example of prescience and radicalism. Demands were made for shorter working days for workers, safety and insurance rules, women's suffrage and the end of child labor. Amongst the more radical elements of the platform were the calls for the collective ownership of land and the financial system, the abolition of the Senate and the end of Judicial Review. Of course many of these policies were later adopted by the Democratic Party and have since come to be seen as obvious structural elements of our society. The appeal for constitutional and economic upheaval, however, never attracted any support amongst the political mainstream.

Despite not winning a single electoral vote, Debs received 901,551 votes, nearly 6% of the total. In eight states; Arizona, California, Idaho, Montana, Nevada, Oklahoma, Oregon and Washington, Debs drew more than 10% of the popular vote. Amongst the four candidates, Debs came in third in Arizona, California, Louisiana and Nevada, beating out Taft, and in Florida and Mississippi, besting Roosevelt. These successes, coupled with the internal division in the Republican Party should have formed the basis for continued growth of the Socialist brand. However, the party's history following the 1912 poll is one of division and decline.

In 1916 Debs refused to run again. The 590,524 votes received by Socialist candidate Allen Bensen proved that, without Debs, the party could not hold onto the liberal voters supporting Wilson whose campaign slogan reminded Americans that he "kept us out" of World War 1. The next year, however, American did enter World War 1. Congress passed the Espionage Act, which made it a crime for a person to convey information with intent to interfere with the operation or success of the armed forces of the United States or to promote the success of its enemies. Political activists of all stripes were prosecuted on charges of violating the act, but the nation's "Red Scare" following the Russian Revolution and violent acts by anarchists, especially the spark that ignited the Great War, the assassination of Archduke Franz Ferdinand, by Gavrilo Princip, made leftists a particularly attractive target.

On June 16, 1918, Debs was arrested following a speech in which he declared that "the master class has always declared the wars, the subject class has always fought the battles; the master class has had all to gain and nothing to lose, while the subject class has had nothing to gain and all to lose – especially their lives." Broadly interpreting the act, Debs was convicted of obstructing the recruitment of soldiers. At his sentencing hearing Debs, speaking to the judge, stated

[y]our Honor, years ago I recognized my kinship with all living beings and I made up my mind that I was not one bit better than the meanest on Earth. I said then, and I say now, that while there is a lower class, I am in it, and while there is a criminal element I am of it, and while there is a soul in prison, I am not free.

Debs received a sentence of ten years in prison and lifetime disenfranchisement.

Debs ran for president in 1920 from prison. Although he received a comparable number of votes to his 1912 tally, this result was little comfort for the party's prospects as women's suffrage between the elections nearly doubled the size of the electorate and meant that Debs barely broke 3% of the total votes cast. Although President Warren G. Harding commuted Debs's sentence in 1921 to time served, Debs did not run again after his release from prison. In 1924 the Socialists endorsed the ad-hoc candidacy of Robert LaFollette's Progressive Party; that party disbanded upon LaFollette's death the following year. Debs's death in 1926 left the party a new perennial candidate, Norman Thomas. Thomas, an articulate and engaging former pastor spent the next six election cycles struggling against the progressive liberalism of Franklin Delano Roosevelt's New Deal and the revival of the Red Scare brought by the Cold War.

Following the Second World War, with labor unions an all but official part of the American economy and society, and the Cold War running from tepid to a near boil, only ideologues and egomaniacs sought to involve themselves in the party. The party fractured and reformed so many times it became difficult to keep score of who was in charge and what factions held sway. Some purists opposed FDR's New Deal and advocated a pro-Soviet foreign policy. Others felt the best way to affect changes was from within the ever more liberal Democratic Party of the 1960s.

Finally the 1968 Democratic Convention in Chicago wrenched the Socialist Party[25] apart, with the conservative "Unity Caucus" led by Max Shachtman and the centrist "Coalition Caucus" led by Michael Harrington inside the convention hall while the radical "Debs Caucus" led by David McReynolds protested outside.

The final straw for the party came during the 1972 Democratic nominating process. The Coalition Caucus stood behind George McGovern, the Democratic nominee, and the Unity Caucus declared their neutrality between McGovern and President Nixon when their candidate, Henry M. "Scoop" Jackson, failed to win the nomination. The Debs Caucus supported the independent candidacy of Benjamin Spock, author of the famed child-rearing books. These factions soon split apart, each taking different names. Today, a core of approximately 1,000 individuals are dues-paying members of a party calling itself the Socialist Party USA, which was formed by remnants of the Debs Caucus after all other factions had ceased using the name "Socialist Party".

Being a doctrinal party, the Socialists could never realize their full potential. However, as far as doctrine goes, socialists and the Socialist Party advocated for broad-based platforms more analogous to latter-day Populists than the Prohibitionists or other pure doctrinal parties. The party lacked a full comprehension of the movement's core appeal. Despite the party's words of industrial solidarity, the party's greatest source of strength came from descendants of Populism in the agrarian west and mid-west. Thus, the party often spoke the words of the factory floor to the farmers and ranchers who provided higher proportions of voters.

Additionally, the party's timing could not have been worse. Continuously beset by standard realignment tactics, first by Wilson and Teddy Roosevelt in 1912,

---

[25] The moniker Socialist Party, while apt, was also a great stretch. In reality it was at this time more of a movement of socialists ranging from essentially New Deal Democrats to full-blown communists.

then later by FDR in the 1930s and 1940s, the Socialists could never fully juxtapose their policies with those of the other major parties. Moreover, leadership and success was often in the hands of a few powerful personalities that rarely countenanced dissent and failed to hold the party together over ideological minutiae. Finally, events in Europe, from anarchists to communists, maintained ample fodder for fear-mongers to cast left-wing and socialist politics as a threat to the American way of life. Put simply, personalities and world events simply got in the way.

Elephants, Donkeys & a Bull Moose:

The Bull Moose Progressive Party

We stand at Armageddon, and we battle for the Lord

– Theodore Roosevelt, 1912

At times in American history, the name "Progressive" has been applied to several political parties of varying stripes. But in the pantheon of Progressive Parties, only one can be said to have played a transformational role in U.S. political history. The Progressive Party as it existed in the 1912 election, popularly known as the Bull Moose Party after its leader, Theodore Roosevelt, responded to doubts about his health by declaring himself "fit as a Bull Moose," caused the end of nearly a half-century of Republican domination in American politics. Roosevelt's larger-than-life personality was a presence in 1912 that also re-crafted presidential election politics. Though unable to emerge as a new major party, the Bull Moose Party managed, in a single year, to utterly realign U.S. party politics and shatter the post-Civil War political status quo.

Theodore Roosevelt ascended to the presidency in 1901 following the assassination of President McKinley less than a year after McKinley's 1900 reelection. The Roosevelt presidency was the perfect beginning to what has been termed The American Century. Roosevelt oversaw numerous domestic reforms, including the establishment of the Food and Drug Administration, but is most remembered for his role in international affairs. Roosevelt rebuilt the U.S. Navy and dispatched the Great White Fleet on a global voyage that announced the arrival of the United States as a great power on the world stage. Roosevelt was responsible for the events that led to the creation of Panama as an independent nation and the construction of the Panama Canal, which allowed the U.S. Navy to be a truly global force. During his administration Roosevelt also negotiated the end of hostilities between Japan and Russia during the 1905 Ruso-Japanese War, a role that earned him the Nobel Peace Prize.

Having served three of the four years to which McKinley was elected, and subsequently being elected in his own right in 1904, Roosevelt opted not to run for reelection in 1908. Instead, Roosevelt hand picked his successor, then Secretary of

War William Howard Taft, by pushing through his nomination in the Republican convention; enjoying Roosevelt's enthusiastic support Taft won by a comfortable margin. Roosevelt's support of Taft was premised on both a personal friendship and Roosevelt's belief that Taft would continue his progressive, reformist policies. This belief proved misplaced and Roosevelt quickly came to regret his decision.

Taft never desired the presidency, instead preferring a seat on the Supreme Court (a position he would eventually attain). Once in the Oval Office Taft aligned himself with conservative elements of the Republican Party in a way that Roosevelt felt betrayed his progressive legacy. When Roosevelt returned to the U.S. after a world-tour of hunting in Africa and public appearances in Europe, the long friendship between Taft and Roosevelt began to fray. Roosevelt became more willing to comment upon and criticize the policies of his successor, first in private and then later in public. Given Roosevelt's colossal popularity and personality, he was impossible to ignore. Eventually Roosevelt, who had previously eschewed a third term, announced his intention to seek the Republican nomination in 1912.

The stark contrast between the men is best exemplified by the nomination that ensued. Roosevelt planned to rely on his immense personal popularity to win the nomination through direct primaries. Taft and his allies, on the other hand, sought to block the use of direct primaries in as many states as possible and secure Taft's nomination through the patronage of party bosses and officeholders. As the nomination process unfolded the acrimony between the two candidates rose and their friendship paid the price.

Taft and Roosevelt resorted to name calling. Taft labeled Roosevelt an "egoist" and a "demagogue," and Roosevelt, for his part, abandoned all decorum and simply spat the epithet "fathead" at the president. Following one campaign speech Taft retreated to his train, slumped into a chair and placed his head in his hands. Taft then wept as he lamented that Roosevelt had once been his closest friend. The next day Roosevelt accused Taft of hypocrisy and disloyalty. Political differences had become personal, and the personal attacks fueled the political contest between the men.

By the time of the nominating convention the rift between Roosevelt and Taft extended throughout the Republican Party. Party bosses managed to steal delegates from Roosevelt by awarding split or contested delegations overwhelmingly to Taft supporters. When defeat looked imminent, Roosevelt's supporters withdrew from the convention. In a swift display of anti-establishment frustration and pro-Roosevelt passions, California's governor, Hiram Johnson, declared that a new party was to be formed for Roosevelt's candidacy.

A hastily assembled convention was organized and Roosevelt was nominated. The convention was a raucous affair, which included the first female delegates to a political party with national prominence. During the convention social activist Jane Addams, in seconding T.R.'s nomination, became the first woman to nominate a candidate for the presidency with a chance of winning. Financial backing for the new party came largely from publishing mogul Frank Munsey and financier George Perkins, both long-time supporters of progressive causes, who also helped craft the party's platform. The Bull Moose platform was the very embodiment of progressive values, calling for labor rights, environmental conservation, women's suffrage, and insurance for the unemployed and the aged.

The Bull Moose nominating convention ushered in a new age in presidential politics. For the first time, a candidate appeared at a major convention to accept the party's nomination. Previously, candidates, even those whose nominations were a *fait accompli*, were not present at conventions, instead awaiting official notice of their nomination. Roosevelt's presence from the start was a dramatic break from the past. His singular dominance at the convention marked an historic shift from which American politics has never reversed course. From now on, presidential campaigns would be candidate-, rather than party-, centered.

With the split in the Republican Party complete, Democrats had good reason to believe they would win the White House in 1912. Democrats had only occuppied the Oval Office thrice since the Civil War: Andrew Johnson's ascension following the assassination of President Lincoln and the two nonconsecutive terms of Grover Cleveland. With such a prize waiting in the wings the Democratic Party's nominating process became highly divisive. Democrats from across the political spectrum and representing various regions of the nation vied for the nomination. On the 46th ballot of a contentious nominating convention, the Democrats selected Woodrow Wilson, governor of New Jersey, as their nominee. The resulting campaign, which included a former president, the incumbent president, a future president, and socialist candidate Eugene V. Debs, was one of the most dynamic in American History.

Social and economic change in the nation, accelerated with advances in transportation and communication technology, fueled fundamental changes in American politics. All four candidates recognized this change and each occupied a distinct position in the socio-political spectrum of ideas and policies responding to this change. Taft was clearly the conservative, representing the status quo, and Debs was nothing less than his polar opposite. Roosevelt and Wilson, however, each put forth their own visions of reform identified as New Nationalism and New Freedom, respectively. Given the mood of the nation, and Taft's virtual disappearance from the campaign trail, the race settled into a contest between the two distinct reformers.

Roosevelt's New Nationalism envisioned a strong governmental role in economic affairs. Roosevelt sought executive, rather than legislative or judicial, regulation of business. For Roosevelt, the president alone possessed a direct link with the people and was their ultimate protector against abuses of power. Wilson, conversely, believed that monopolistic enterprises could not be sufficiently regulated. For Wilson, such views logically led to the dismantling of trusts rather than their regulation. On the campaign trail Wilson warned that New Nationalism would result in economic collectivism whereby corporations and government would wield far too much power.

New Nationalism suffered from an inherent paradox in the Progressive Bull Moose platform. Aggrandized national regulatory powers could not easily be reconciled with the simultaneous calls for popular rule through direct democracy. These competing forces, necessarily diametrically opposed to one another, could not easily be bridged, and the result was the opening of a large field in which Wilson could compete. Advocates of Wilson's New Freedom found substantial middle-ground in which to present their vision for American government with expanded national powers absent bureaucratic centralization. Both candidates could claim a reformist mantle. The question came down to New Nationalism's aggressive use of government versus New Freedom's emphasis on individualism, both appealing to progressives.

The birth of Wilson's New Freedom came over a lunch between himself and future Supreme Court Justice Louis D. Brandeis, then a Boston lawyer known as "the people's attorney." Wilson knew that should the campaign become a contest of personalities he would lose, and so he had to find an issue upon which to attack Roosevelt. It was Brandeis who convinced Wilson that *the* issue had to be the trusts. By crusading to destroy these monopolies rather than regulate them, Brandeis argued, Wilson could become a populist progressive on the economic issues of the day. After the meeting with Brandeis, Wilson found his voice in the campaign and was able to meet Roosevelt on a more level playing field. Simply put,

Wilson said, the election was one between a "program of Liberty" and a "program of regulation."

Roosevelt responded by attacking Wilson as a disingenuous progressive. After Wilson declared that "the history of liberty is a history of the limitation of governmental power, not the increase of it," Roosevelt responded by declaring that limiting government in the face of new economic realities would lead to "the enslavement of the people." It was Roosevelt's belief that nothing short of the exercise of federal power was the sole means to reign in the powers of big business.

In the campaign between Roosevelt and Wilson can be heard the echoes of Jefferson and Hamilton's struggle to define the character of the nation in its early days. Wilson's belief in limited government and economic competition between small enterprises harkened back to Jefferson's harsh critique of federal power and his emphasis on local rule. Roosevelt, on the other hand, channeled Alexander Hamilton's commitment to strong central government as the supreme arbiter of economic matters.

Interestingly, the same fears and accusations that surrounded Hamilton were cast at Roosevelt. Journalistic attacks painted Roosevelt as a new Caesar, seeking to destroy the republic and impose his own imperium. One attack claimed that Roosevelt's election would bring "the end of the Republic and the beginning of a Dictatorship." Regardless of the sensibility and veracity of these claims, it further cast the two campaigns in very traditional Jeffersonian-Hamiltonian terms. That a third party should be a standard-bearer in this classic question of national power and identity further demonstrates how substantial was the role of Roosevelt's Progressive Bull Moose candidacy in realigning the political landscape of America, and how insignificant was the candidacy of the incumbent president. That the outcome of this contest was not a new major party only highlights the great difficulties facing new political movements in the United States.

In the closing days of the campaign Roosevelt began to adopt many positions first articulated by Wilson in the hope of winning over progressive Democrats, especially a call for economic competition. When this failed, Roosevelt looked to progressive Republicans; however, there were too few to guarantee victory. Roosevelt's hopes had to be pinned on his personal stature and cult of personality. The living legend of Roosevelt was aided greatly in one of the most bizarre and incredible occurrences in American presidential campaign history.

On October 14, Roosevelt was on his way to deliver a speech in Milwaukee, Wisconsin. Having recently exhausted himself with the herculean pace of his campaign schedule, Roosevelt was urged to take a break from the campaign, but the indefatigable Roosevelt refused, only agreeing to extra police protection to help hold back the crowds that would inevitably throng the candidate. This protection proved inadequate for the real threat awaiting Roosevelt.

Riding to the auditorium, Roosevelt's car was met with cheering crowds. As Roosevelt rose to greet the crowd, a fanatic shouting out against a third-term presidency approached Roosevelt and fired a single shot from a Colt revolver. Roosevelt was shot in the chest, his shirt soaked with blood. Incredibly, Roosevelt insisted on delivering his speech before he would agree to any medical attention, proclaiming, "You get me to the speech. It may be the last one I shall ever deliver, but I am going to deliver this one."

Inside the auditorium doctors inspected Roosevelt as he was preparing for the speech. Doctors again urged Roosevelt to go to a hospital. Roosevelt simply stated, "I will deliver this speech or die, one or the other." Roosevelt went on to deliver his speech in full, which lasted for nearly an hour! In opening his remarks Roosevelt acknowledged what had just taken place:

> Friends, I shall ask you to be as quiet as possible. I don't know whether you fully understand that I have just been shot; but it takes more than that to kill a Bull Moose... The bullet is in

114

me now, so that I cannot make a very long speech, but I will try my best.

The Bull Moose Party and Roosevelt earned their moniker that evening. After the speech Roosevelt was rushed to the hospital for treatment. He recovered quickly, and following the incident received such favorable coverage in the press that Roosevelt believed the assassination attempt might be just the thing to turn the election in his favor.

During Roosevelt's recuperation Taft and Wilson suspended their campaigns. Incredibly, Roosevelt and the campaign were back in full swing within a week! In back-to-back appearances at Madison Square Garden in New York City, Roosevelt and Wilson addressed rapturous crowds. Roosevelt's speech, delivered October 30, was delayed nearly forty-five minutes by the cheering crowd that came out to see him. Wilson's supporters, gathered the next day, bested those of Roosevelt by nearly fifteen minutes, refusing to allow Wilson to begin for over an hour with their ecstatic applause.

The Madison Square Garden appearances marked a perfect capstone to the campaign. It had come down to these two candidates and the election results reflected this. Wilson was the victor with 6,296,284 votes to Roosevelt's 4,122,721. Taft, unsurprisingly, came in third with less than three-and-a-half million votes. Debs rounded out the election capturing slightly more than 900,000 votes. Nevertheless, these results translated into a landside for Wilson in the Electoral College. Wilson carried 40 states for 435 electoral votes. Roosevelt captured only six states, garnering 88 votes in the Electoral College. Taft managed to eke out the states of Utah and Vermont, yielding only four electoral votes each.

As the Bull Moose campaign was essentially centered on Roosevelt the man, few other Bull Moose candidates for office fared well, and the Progressives ended up with only one senate seat and nine members in the House. Nontheless, the Progressive Bull Moose Party realigned national politics in a way that gave birth to the modern American system. For one, the candidate-centered campaign is a staple of the modern campaign Americans have grown to expect. Without the force of personality of Roosevelt, the very basis upon which the Progressive Bull Moose Party was able to form, it is hard to imagine the circumstances and personalities that would have given rise to this phenomenon until at least the advent of the modern media age still decades away.

Additionally, the election cast the Republican Party as the conservative party of the status quo, whereas the Democratic Party was able to shift into the progressive camp. This transformation of party identity is a complete one-hundred-eighty degree turnaround from the political dynamic as it existed in the lead-up and aftermath of the Civil War. Further realigning the political landscape, Wilson, though governor of New Jersey, was born in Virginia and raised in Georgia, making him the first southern president since Zachary Taylor's election in 1848.

With the rupture in the Republican Party and the advent of the Bull Moose Party, the Democrats were also able to win in states that had previously been reliably Republican since Abraham Lincoln's election in 1860. Though the Democratic Party continued to count the Southern United States as its bastion of support until the Civil Rights Era again up-ended America's political map, Woodrow Wilson was able to capture and retain the presidency as a national candidate.

Beyond the immediate consequences of the 1912 election, however, is the role Roosevelt and the Bull Moose Party played in setting the stage for the future political dynamic of the United States. Upon his inauguration, Wilson was forced to recognize the popularity of TR's brand of progressive politics, as well as the support garnered by Taft; consequently, Wilson governed much more as a New Nationalist, abandoning much of the decentralized vision of his New Freedom agenda.

The 1912 election was both the beginning and the beginning of the end of the Bull Moose Party. Following the 1914 mid-term elections the Bull Moose Party dropped to six seats in the U.S. House of Representatives, though Hiram Johnson, originally elected as a Republican, managed reelection as governor of California while running as a Progressive Bull Moose. By 1916 the party was over, literally and figuratively – TR declined a second run as the party's candidate and eventually went back to the Republican Party, though the party was now securely run by its conservative elements and remains so.

The full manifestation of the realignment in national governance and politics brought by the Bull Moose Party would be realized by another Roosevelt – Franklin Delano. Under FDR, not only did the preceding Republican dominance give way to Democratic rule for more than a generation, but the exercise of executive power for regulation and administration of the national economy shifted into high gear. The realignment begun by one Roosevelt under New Nationalism was completed by another Roosevelt, entitled the New Deal.

Right From the Left:
The American Independent Party

"There's not a dime's worth of difference between the Democrat and Republican Parties."

– Alabama Gov. George C. Wallace

When looking at the 1968 presidential election, students of American political history understandably think more of the strife and violence that roiled the nation than they consider one of the twentieth century's most significant third parties. The great Civil Rights leader, the Reverend Martin Luther King, Jr., was slain in Memphis that year. Following King's assassination, riots broke out throughout the country in urban centers large and small. Later that year, while campaigning for the Democratic nomination for president, U.S. Senator Robert Kennedy, brother of assassinated president John F. Kennedy, was shot and killed. To cap off the drama of that year, the 1968 Democratic Party Nominating Convention in Chicago witnessed violent clashes between police and protesters.

With such riveting events taking place in quick succession it is easy to understand why third party politics in 1968 may be relegated to mere footnotes or forgotten altogether. However, it was these same social and political upheavals taking place in the United States that allowed for the emergence of the American Independent Party. This third party, though as short lived as any explored herein, is one of the most impactful of the twentieth century, and one whose presence in American history continues to resonate today. The American Independent Party, the role it played in the 1968 election, and how American politics was firmly realigned by its presence is vital to understanding U.S. politics to the present day.

The American Independent Party provides an exemplary modern-day illustration of the challenges facing third parties. While the party achieved significant ballot access, it could do so only after herculean effort and proactive strategic planning. The party also demonstrates the lasting appeal of alternative politics in the United States; in many ways, The American Independent Party was the successor to Strom Thurmond's Dixiecrats in 1948 and engaged many of the same issues and voters. The American Independent Party also displays the great irony of third party politics in the United States; the closer the party came to achieving the improbable, the more vulnerable it was to the efforts of the major parties to label it a spoiler. The American Independent Party in the 1968 election is truly illuminating to those who wish to understand American politics today, third party or otherwise.

The American Independent Party was the brainchild of one man: Alabama Governor George C. Wallace. Wallace may best be remembered for one of the most memorable and revolting political rallying cries of the twentieth century. Taking the oath of office as the newly elected governor of Alabama, and standing on the very spot where, over a century before, Jefferson Davis was sworn in as President of the Confederate States of America, Wallace declared that he was entering the governor's mansion to ensure "segregation today, segregation tomorrow, segregation forever!"[26] Thankfully, Wallace's stand against Civil Rights could not stem the tide of freedom and equality sweeping the nation during the 1960s.

The Civil Rights movement received a significant boost when President Truman integrated the U.S. armed forces with Executive Order 9981 in 1948. From this single act, the Democratic Party began a slow but inextricable shift ever more firmly into the Civil Rights camp. Under Democratic president Lyndon B. Johnson, Civil Rights became a central component of Democratic politics, even if not all Democratic elected officials supported this position. This political shift helped to complete a realigning transformation of the major parties; whereas the Democratic Party had previously been the Southern reactionary, segregationist party dating back to before the Civil War, now it was increasingly gaining support in Northern states and embraced a progressive stance in favor of Civil Rights.

---

[26] Wallace later sought to turn these words into action when he stood in the doorway of the Foster Auditorium at the University of Alabama on June 11, 1963 in an attempt to block the entry of two black students, Vivian Malone Jones and James Hood.

In response to these changes, Wallace broke with the Democratic Party and forged a nation-wide coalition of conservative whites under the banner of his newly formed American Independent Party. Wallace embraced both reactionary segregationist politics as well as mainstream socio-political positions. Consequently, Wallace's new party posed a threat not only to the Democratic Party from which he broke ranks; Wallace threatened the entirety of the political establishment, Democrat and Republican alike.

In the industrial North, Wallace appealed to blue-collar Democrats. These northern, working-class Democrats had had enough of the protests and tumult raging throughout the country. Wallace spoke to their anger when he inveighed against the disorder seen to be caused by racial minorities, protesting students, and an intellectual elite out of touch with mainstream Americans. Democratic voters who felt abandoned or ignored by the Democratic Party they traditionally supported flocked to Wallace. Wallace promised "law and order" to this constituency. These same voters would later be labeled "Reagan Democrats" when they again left the Democratic Party in the 1980 presidential election.

In the South, Wallace's call for law and order also resonated. With his passionate segregationist position, he threatened Nixon's appeal to Southern whites who also felt the Democratic Party had long since abandoned them but who had not yet fully embraced the Republican Party. By 1968 Southern white voters had only recently ended their long-held allegiance to the Democratic Party and were not reliable, habitual Republican voters. Further mitigating the seemingly obvious migration of Southern white voters from the Democratic Party to the Republican Party was the fact that Nixon accepted the Supreme Court's 1954 *Brown v. Board of Education of Topeka* decision.[27] Nixon's attempt to reap the benefits of both worlds in the Civil rights struggle by simultaneously staking out a position against the

---

[27] 347 U.S. 483, 74 S. Ct. 686;, 98 L. Ed. 873 (1954)

Johnson Administration's implementation of school integration failed to win over pro-Civil Rights whites or satisfy segregationists. An opportunity existed for Wallace and the American Independent Party to exploit the gap that emerged between both parties and their otherwise likely voters.

Wallace's timing and rhetoric perfectly fit the circumstances; his support for the segregationist status quo could be seen as calming pragmatism by the center and sufficiently uncompromising by opponents of Civil Rights. Due to its broad appeal to both Republicans and Democrats, and the geographic breadth enjoyed by his candidacy, Wallace came remarkably close to unsettling the entrenched duopoly in a way not seen since the Republican Party emerged as a major party over 100 years before. However, Wallace still needed to appear on the ballot in order to capture the votes of his supporters.

Wallace's electoral prospects were given a boost by his early decision to enlist a legal team to ensure nation-wide ballot access. The great obstacle faced by so many potential third parties was addressed early and successfully. Wallace eventually attained ballot access in all 50 states. Despite having a team dedicated to navigating the individual state election laws, Wallace's success in this labyrinthine legal morass only came as a result of a Supreme Court case[28] and the need to resort to a variety of party labels, such as the Courage Party in New York, the Conservative Party in Kansas and the aptly named George Wallace Party in Connecticut, amongst others. Wallace and the American Independent Party only failed to appear on the ballot in Washington, D.C., which likely did nothing to hurt his overall election prospects as his campaign was unlikely to have had much resonance with that city's electorate. The challenges to ballot access that Wallace and the American Independent Party overcame, and the contortions into which they

---

[28] *Williams v. Rhodes*, 393 U.S. 23, 89 S. Ct. 5, 21 L. Ed. 2d 24 (1968). This case brought together the American Independent Party and the Socialist Labor Party together as plaintiffs. Politics surely does make for strange bedfellows, and third party politics even more so.

were forced are the same as those faced by all modern third parties, no matter how successful they may ultimately be.

One damaging paradox to Wallace's wide appeal is the fact that both campaigns could implore their otherwise natural voters to eschew Wallace for fear of electing the other major party candidate by splitting the vote. Again, The American Independent Party acutely demonstrates the risk faced by all third parties, that of being seen as a spoiler, and thus handing the election to the greater of two evils. Only in 1968 this hazard was doubly present. After enjoying a strong early campaign, Wallace's support began to collapse as election day approached. Voters returned to the familiar Democratic and Republican Parties for fear of handing the election to the other.

While Wallace never presumed he would capture the White House, he had good reason to believe he could cause a hung Electoral College and exact concessions. This strategy was also Strom Thurmond's aim when he broke with the Democrats to run as a Dixiecrat twenty years earlier. Yet Wallace's plan was thwarted by a great realignment within the Republican Party. Caused almost entirely by the threat from Wallace and the American Independent Party, the Republican Party charted a new political and rhetorical course, which they have only recently, though not entirely, abandoned. Due to the American Independent Party's strong appeal to Southern whites and outspoken rejection of integration, Nixon's campaign and the Republican Party adopted what became known as "the Southern Strategy."

The Southern United States had long been a bastion of Democratic political dominance. That position eroded as the Democratic Party increasingly embraced the Civil Rights Movement as their own. While these voters were still in flux, the Republican Party risked losing them to the newly emerged and stridently anti-integration American Independent Party. In response, Nixon and the GOP began to adopt the language of "states rights" much as the Dixiecrats had done in 1948. This language appealed to those voters who wanted to prevent federal intervention to end Jim Crow in the former Confederacy, and helped close the gap between Nixon and Wallace. Nixon's plan proved successful in 1968 and for the Republican Party for more than a generation.

When the results were in, Nixon and his Democratic opponent, Hubert Humphrey, polled incredibly close – Nixon beat Humphrey by a mere 517,777 votes out of a total of more than nearly 73 million ballots cast. Wallace captured almost 10 million votes. Nonetheless, Nixon secured the presidency in the Electoral College by a commanding 301 electoral votes to Humphrey's 191.[29] Wallace, however, made an impressive showing by capturing five states and with them 45 electoral votes.[30]

More important than the election results is a breakdown of the state-by-state results to understand how meaningful Wallace's candidacy was. In 21 states, representing 200 votes in the Electoral College, Wallace's vote tally was larger than the difference between Nixon and Humphrey. Additionally, in New York, Wallace's vote total, when combined with all other third parties appearing on the ballot, also surpassed the difference between the two major party candidates, bringing the total impact of third parties in 1968 to 243 electoral votes, out of a total of 538, where 270 were needed to win!

The American Independent Party, despite its impressive performance, virtually disappeared after 1968. More so than even Roosevelt's Bull Moose Progressive Party or La Follette's latter-day Progressives, the American Independent Party truly was a vehicle for one man. By 1972, Wallace was back in the Democratic fold vying for that year's presidential nomination. Without its leader,

---

[29] Nixon originally captured enough states to guarantee 302 votes in the Electoral College, but one elector from North Carolina defected to Wallace.

[30] Plus the additional vote from the faithless elector from North Carolina.

or any other significant popular figure, the party faded to irrelevance. Nonetheless, Wallace remained a popular force to be reckoned with even without his own political party.

During the 1972 Democratic primary campaign Wallace racked up impressive primary wins, taking important prizes like Florida and Michigan. Ultimately though, a bullet fired from a young radical named Arthur Bremer ended Wallace's hopes for presidential glory; Wallace was paralyzed and so were his political aspirations. Remaining American Independent Party members urged Wallace to continue his quest for the White House as the candidate of the party he founded, but he declined.

The candidate the American Independent Party selected, Republican Congressman John Schmitz veered the party from its bipartisan though conservative appeal to a hard right ideology. Notwithstanding Schmitz's impressive showing in 1972, capturing over one million votes, it was clear that most of Wallace's supporters had gravitated to Nixon. Following the 1972 election, the American Independent Party fractured into the American Independent Party and the American Party. Former Georgia governor Lester Maddox ran under the American Independent Party banner and Schmitz's former vice-presidential running mate, Thomas Anderson, ran as the American Party candidate. Neither candidate obtained even one-tenth of one percent of the vote. The party was over.

The American Independent Party failed to outlive its founder, but its impact did not. The Republican Southern Strategy was the response to Wallace's popularity among Southern white voters. The Southern Strategy continued through the twentieth century and led to the firm realignment of southern states to the Republican Party and the shift of black voters, en masse, from the Party of Lincoln to the Democratic Party. The realignment that Nixon brought to the GOP as a response to Wallace also remains salient for today's Democratic Party decades after the 1968 election. Black Americans overwhelmingly vote Democratic and the Republican Party suffers from the taint of being a party for old, white men. With the increased diversity of America's changing demographics, this perception could lead to a systemic advantage for the Democratic Party in the near term.

The legacy of touting States' Rights, which originated in Strom Thurmond's Dixiecrat candidacy in 1948 thus passed from Democratic defectors to the GOP. Despite the seeming congruity between Wallace's break with the Democratic Party and his socio-political stance in 1968 and Strom Thurmond's Dixicrat campaign twenty years earlier, Wallace and the American Independent Party failed to attract prominent political figures to their cause, including Thurmond himself. Perhaps the reason these two perfect political allies did not join forces in 1968 was as karmic as it was political. Wallace did not abandon the Democratic Party to back Thurmond in 1948, and Thurmond did not leave his newly adopted party, the Republicans, in 1968 to support essentially the same platform under Wallace. Had Wallace opted to join Thurmond in 1948, the segregationists may have grown into a successful, albeit sickening, political force over the ensuing twenty years and further altered the course of United States history as we know it.

In 1980, then-Republican presidential nominee Ronald Reagan launched his campaign with a speech lauding states' rights. While some defenders of Reagan claim the inclusion of the phrase was an allusion to his libertarian economic philosophy, the speech was given a few miles from the site of the infamous 1964 murder of Civil Rights activists in Philadelphia, Mississippi. Whatever the motive behind the language and location of this speech, it is certain that it resonated with Thurmond and Wallace supporters from 1948 and 1968, respectively. The American Independent Party could have been to the Dixiecrats what the Republican Party was to the Liberty and Free Soil Parties. Instead, though, the all-too-familiar

126

cooption of this third party's positions by a major party and the systemic impediments to third parties relegate the American Independent Party to a fleeting though significant role in third party history, rather than a permanent role on the national stage.

Left & Right ... But Out:

Third Parties in the Twentieth Century

The 1912 presidential election represents a significant milestone in third party politics in America. At no other time in American history have **two** third parties fared so well. As has been noted, the Debs and Roosevelt candidacies outpolled the sitting president in nearly every race, with Debs even trumping Roosevelt in two contests. For advocates of greater choice amongst political parties in the United States, then and today, 1912 cuts the image of the ideal blueprint for competitive multi-party politics in the United States. It is surprising then that the 1912 election can also be seen as the last gasp of assertive, viable third party politics in the nation for the ensuing century. Only George Wallace in 1968, and H. Ross Perot in 1992 posed a serious challenge to the Republican-Democratic duopoly again in national politics.

Depending on one's perspective, several notable candidates, parties and campaigns pepper the political landscape of the twentieth century. However, few really rise to the level of significance or impact that marks the parties featured in this book. No party ushered in any revolution in the political process as the Anti-Masons had, or emerged as a permanent national force as the Liberty-Free Soil-Republican Party succeeded in doing. No third party of the twentieth or twenty-first centuries espoused any singular doctrinal vision that was later co-opted by a major party and eventually adopted as policy. No, the late twentieth and early twenty-first centuries have been shockingly barren of noteworthy third parties. The Golden Age of third parties seems firmly a thing of the past.

Several reasons exist for the relative absence of significant third parties in the United States in the years between the 1912 election and Wallace's and Perot's runs for the White House. From World War 1 through the Second World War the body politic was firmly ossified into those who were for and those who were against the party in power, reinforcing the two-party system during those years. The extremes of world wars, the Roaring Twenties and the Great Depression, buttressed the American political dichotomy. After Wilson and World War I, the country returned to the Republican dominance that had been virtually uninterrupted since the Civil War.

When times were good, voters were content with the *status quo*. When the Great Depression struck, however, a new coalition of voters was formed that finished the realignment begun by Wilson; an era of Democratic dominance began with FDR's New Deal and lasted into the Civil Rights era. While the struggle for Civil Rights shifted political loyalties and eventually ended Democratic supremacy, the Cold War essentially kept voters firmly within the two-party system. Only once during the entire Cold War, with George Wallace's American Independent Party, did the static Cold War dichotomy truly face a threat, and this aberration occurred due to the temporary elevation of domestic concerns over international affairs in the post-war period.

Notable parties and candidacies did appear during this time, however. Senator Robert "fighting Bob" La Follette of Wisconsin claimed the mantle of Progressivism in 1924 to run for president. As has been noted, in 1948 Senator Strom Thurmond, running as a Dixiecrat,[31] sought to deny President Truman an outright majority in the Electoral College, thus resorting to a vote in the House of Representatives where Dixiecrats hoped to weaken the Democratic Party's Civil Rights platform planks.

La Follette had challenged both Taft and Roosevelt for the 1912 Republican nomination. La Follette, however made little impact in his 1924 bid. For one, La Follette emerged out of another failed bid to run as the Republican candidate for

---

[31] The term "Dixiecrat" is a portmanteau of *Dixie*, referring to the Southern United States, and *Democrat*, referring to the Democratic Party.

president.   Unlike, Teddy Roosevelt, though, La Follette lacked the personal following and national appeal that aided Roosevelt in launching the Bull Moose Progressive Party. La Follette was cross-endorsed by the rapidly declining Socialists and even ran as a Socialist in some states where his Progressive Party failed to gain ballot access. His candidacy, however, failed ot make any lasting impact worthy of inclusion here.

While La Follette and Thurmond represent interesting and esoteric chapters of American political history, they do not rise to the level of relevance germane to the scope of this work. Surely they are of interest to the readers, and certainly the writer, of this book, but they fail to satisfy the basic standards established for inclusion in their own chapter.

Left, Right & Center ... But Still Out:
Third Parties Today

Give Me Libertarianism or Give Me Death: The Libertarian Party

"Extremism in the defense of liberty is no vice. Moderation in the pursuit of justice is no virtue."

– Barry Goldwater (1964)

The birth of the United States was the culmination of an evolution in thinking that has been termed The Enlightenment. Sparked by the revolutionary thinking of illuminaries such as René Descartes and Isaac Newton, who emphasized systematic thinking in philosophy and science, the Enlightnment cast off the traditions and superstitions of the Middle Ages. Throughout the 18th Century radical thinkers like John Stuart Mill, Voltaire, Jean-Jacques Rousseau, and David Hume questioned and attacked the institutional status quo of Church and State.

America had its own radicals, most perfectly personified in Thomas Paine, who penned *Common Sense*, the incendiary call for American Independence, in 1776. In time the thinking spawned by Enlightenment philosophers morphed into libertarianism, whose adherants would go on to found the Libertarian Party. The Libertarian Party is currently the largest third party in the United States, claiming over 200,000 registered voters and over 600 elected officials nation-wide; it has more people in public office than all other third parties combined.

The political platform of the Libertarian Party reflects the group's particular brand of libertarianism, favoring minimally regulated, *laissez-faire* markets, strong defense of civil liberties, and non-interventionism in foreign policy that respects freedom of trade and travel to all foreign countries. These positions obviously speak to a doctrinal foundation; however, unlike other doctrinal parties the Libertarian Party's doctrinaire stance is tied to a political philosophy rather than a single issue as has been the case with its doctrinal third party brethren.

Due to its relatively recent origins, it is impossible to determine whether the Libertarian Party will have the same impact that many other doctrinal parties have enjoyed. Further, the Libertarian Party, with its broad issue and policy platform, could prove, in time, to play a role in some future realignment of the U.S. political landscape, especially if some of the more libertarian leaning Tea Party activists find themselves dissatisfied within the Republican Party as it exists today.

However, due to some unique characteristics of this current third party it merits more than mere passing mention. Of particular note has been the high profile of many Libertarian Party Candidates, including former members of congress, and a unique phenomenon in American political hisotry – The Free State Project – that, while not formally associated with the Libertarian Party cannot be seen as anything other than a libertarian activist movement.

The Libertarian Party was formed in the home of David Nolan in 1971 after several months of debate among members of the Committee to Form a Libertarian Party. This group included John Hospers, Edward Crane, and Murray Rothbard, all of whom played significant roles in the formation of the political philosophy of the American brand of libertarianism and the Libertarian Party; Hospers would eventually run for the President on the Libertarian ticket and Crane founded the Cato Institute, the highly influential libertarian think-tank.

The party's founders were heavily influenced by the thinking of indivduals such as Thomas Paine and the anarchist Pierre-Joseph Proudhon, and the Objectivist views of theorist and author Ayn Rand. Proudhoun was the first to use the term "libertarian" in his writings, and though she sought to distance herself from the label "libertarian," Rand, and her works, *The Fountainhead* and *Atlas Shrugged*, have inspired countless libertarians. Proudhoun described his views on government in his essay *What is Government* in which he said,

> [t]o be governed is to be watched, inspected, spied upon, directed, law-driven, numbered, regulated, enrolled, indoctrinated, preached at, controlled, checked, estimated, valued, censured, commanded, by creatures who have neither the right nor the wisdom nor the virtue to do so. To be governed is to be at every operation, at every transaction noted, registered, counted, taxed, stamped, measured, numbered, assessed, licensed, authorized, admonished, prevented, forbidden, reformed, corrected, punished. It is, under pretext of public utility, and in the name of the general interest, to be place[d] under

contribution, drilled, fleeced, exploited, monopolized, extorted from, squeezed, hoaxed, robbed; then, at the slightest resistance, the first word of complaint, to be repressed, fined, vilified, harassed, hunted down, abused, clubbed, disarmed, bound, choked, imprisoned, judged, condemned, shot, deported, sacrificed, sold, betrayed; and to crown all, mocked, ridiculed, derided, outraged, dishonored. That is government; that is its justice; that is its morality.

Though extreme and anarchic, readers of Proudhoun can see the seeds of libertarian aversion to government. This loathing of governmental power and the perceived intrusion into private and financial life would spawn many followers and schools of thought, one of which was to become the Libertarian Party.

Prompted in part by price controls and the end of the Gold Standard implemented by President Richard Nixon, the founding members of Libertarian Party viewed the dominant Republican and Democratic parties as having diverged from what they viewed as the libertarian principles of America's Founding Fathers. A press conference announcing the new party was held in January 1972, and the first national convention, attracting 89 delegates from 23 states, was held in June in Denver, Colorado.

Even before the party's formal creation, the libertarian activists had reason for optimism. The Florida Libertarian Party, founded in 1970, achieved an early victory, a popular initiative, and Miguel Gilson-De Lemos was elected in a partisan local board race in New York even before the adoption of the party's first platform. This optimism was quickly tempered, however. In subsequent years the number of Libertarians in office seems to be holding steady at about 1% of its donor base. Libertarians could count approximately 30 officeholders with 3,000 donors in 1981; 100 in office and 10,000 donors in 1991; and 600 elected or appointed officials compared to 60,000 donors in 2001.

By the 1972 presidential election, the party had grown to over 80 members and had attained ballot access in two states, Colorado and Washington. Their presidential ticket, John Hospers and Theodora Nathan, earned fewer than 3,000 votes, but received the first and only electoral college vote for a Libertarian presidential ticket, from Roger MacBride of Virginia, who was pledged to Richard Nixon. MacBride's vote was also the first vote ever cast for a woman in the United States Electoral College. In 1976, MacBride became the party's presidential nominee, and the Libertarian party achieved ballot access in 32 states.

Following the 1976 election the party saw a series of small, but symbolically significant successes. In 1978 Dick Randolph became the first Libertarian to win state-level office with his election to the Alaska House of Representatives. Randolph was reelected in 1980 and was instrumental in the adoption of a major libertarian initiative, the repeal of the state income tax. Going into the 1980 presidential contest, the Libertarian Party gained ballot access in all 50 states, the District of Columbia, and the U.S. territory of Guam, the first time a third party accomplished this since the Socialist Party in 1916. The ticket of Ed Clark and David H. Koch spent several million dollars on this political campaign and earned nearly one million votes, more than one percent of the popular vote, the most successful Libertarian presidential campaign to date.

On December 29, 1981, the first widely reported successful election in the continental United States of a Libertarian Party candidate in a partisan race occurred as Richard P. Siano, a Boeing 707 pilot for Trans World Airlines, running against both a Republican and a Democrat, was elected to the office of Kingwood Township Committeeman in western Hunterdon County, New Jersey. His election resulted from a special election held to break a tie vote in the general election between him and the Democratic candidate. He received 63% of the votes cast in the special election and served a three-year term in office.

Despite the track record of growth, the Libertarian Party suffered a major setback when, in 1983, the party was divided by internal disputes. Former party leaders Edward Crane and David Koch left, taking a number of their supporters with them. In the 1984 election, the party's presidential nominee, David Bergland, gained ballot access in only 36 states and earned one-quarter of one percent of the popular vote. Nonetheless, the Libertarian Party could still count the occasional grass-roots success. In 1987, Doug Anderson became the first Libertarian elected to office in a major city, elected to the Denver Election Commission; later, in 2005, Anderson was elected to the Lakewood, Colorado city council.

In 1988, the profile and the prospects for the Libertarian Party took a markedly positive turn. In that year, former Republican Congressman Ron Paul won the Libertarian nomination for president and was on the ballot in 46 states. Paul later successfully ran again for United States House of Representatives from Texas, once again as a Republican.[32] Congressman Paul's brand of conservatism and his libertarian leanings were again put on national display during the 2008 Republican presidential primaries and many called for him to run as a Libertarian when he failed to capture the Republican nomination. Despite this support Paul chose to focus on libertarian activism while remaining in the Republican Party.

Following his withdrawal from the primary campaign, Paul launched a new political action and advocacy group called the Campaign for Liberty. The stated goal of the Campaign for Liberty is to "spread the message of the Constitution and limited government, while at the same time organizing at the grassroots level and teaching pro-liberty activists how to run effective campaigns and win elections at every level of government." Again, it is impossible to tell the ultimate long-term effects of this movement and whether it will carry the banner of the Libertarian

---

[32] In his 2008 and 2012 bids for the Republican presidential nomination Paul clearly carved out a niche for himself as the "libertarian" candidate in a field of more traditional conservatives of various persuasions.

Party in years to come. The picture is cloudier still with the advent of the Tea Party activists within and without the Republican Party. Knowing which party label they or any candidates may choose is anybody's guess at this point.

In 1992, Andre Marrou, another Libertarian elected to the Alaska state legislature, and Ron Paul's running mate in 1988, led the party's presidential ticket, with attorney Nancy Lord as his Vice Presidential running mate. For the first time since the Clark campaign in 1980, the Libertarian Party made the ballot in all 50 states, DC, and Guam. Nonetheless, this access did not translate into a higher vote count. Most likely due to the presence of Ross Perot's lively independent candidacy in 1992, the Libertarian ticket failed to capture even 300,000 votes in the 1992 election.

In 1994, radio personality Howard Stern embarked on a political campaign for Governor of New York, formally announcing his candidacy under the Libertarian Party ticket. Although he legally qualified for the office and campaigned for a time after his nomination, many viewed the run for office as nothing more than a publicity stunt. Stern subsequently withdrew his candidacy because he did not want to comply with the financial disclosure requirements for candidates.

During subsequent election cycles the Libertarian party managed to maintain nearly complete ballot access throughout the country. Harry Browne, who headed the 1996 and 2000 presidential tickets, enjoyed access in all 50 states, DC and Guam in 1996, and made the ballot in 49 states, DC and Guam in 2000. In 2000, however, the Arizona Libertarian Party, which had disaffiliated from the national organization in late 1999, but which still controlled the Libertarian ballot line in that state, nominated science fiction author L. Neil Smith and newspaperman

Vin Suprynowicz, rather than Browne and his running mate, Art Olivier, as its presidential slate. Smith and Suprynowicz polled 5,775 votes (0.38%) in Arizona.[33]

In 2004, Michael Badnarik secured the Libertarian Party nomination in the closest Libertarian nomination race to date, in which all candidates finished within two percentage points of each other in the first round of balloting. This result could evidence a growing vibrancy within the party, or could lead to the schisms seen in former third parties that have ultimately led to their demise. Upon winning the nomination, Badnarik also enjoyed widespread ballot access, appearing on the ballot in 48 states, D.C. and Guam, and his candidacy was able to capture nearly 400,000 votes. Despite less name recognition and a much smaller campaign budget, Badnarik polled nearly as well as the much more well-known, and somewhat infamous, independent candidate, Ralph Nader. The Libertarian Party also garnered more votes than the Green Party that year. In 2008, the Libertarian Party nominated former Republican congressman Bob Barr. Like Ron Paul twenty years earlier, Barr, as a former member of Congress, helped draw media attention to the Libertarian Party's campaign. In particular Barr was, for a time during the 1990s, a household name in America, famous for his leading role in the Impeachment hearings of President Bill Clinton. This fact again helped lend substantial name recognition to the Libertarian ticket.

Consistent ballot access and name recognition may prove to be a successful path to success for the Libertarian Party. With the exception of Martin Van Buren's run as the Free Soil candidate and Teddy Roosevelt's Bull Moose campaign, candidate name recognition greatly distinguishes the Libertarian Party from other historical and contemporary third parties who have often seen their hopes and fortunes thwarted by the simple inability to present themselves to voters

---

[33] Interestingly, Browne won a majority of the vote in the town of Searsburg, Vermont (pop. 96) in the 2000 election.

as electable. In time, such individual name recognition may result in party brand recognition and ultimately decide the fate of the Libertarian Party.

Name recognition through ballot access has not been limited to Libertarian presidential candidates. In recent elections, Libertarians have run far more candidates for office, at all levels, than all other third parties combined. In the 2004 elections, 377 Libertarian candidates vied for state legislative seats, compared with 108 Constitution Party candidates, 94 Green Party candidates, and 11 Reform Party candidates. In the 2000 elections, the party ran over 1,400 candidates at the local, state, and federal level. More than 1,600 Libertarians ran for office in the 2002 mid-term election. Accordingly, their combined vote totals have far exceeded those of other parties: in the 2000, 2002, and 2004 elections, Libertarian candidates for the House of Representatives received more than a million votes -- more than twice the votes received by all other minor parties combined in those years.

Possibly the greatest impact of the Libertarian party is not even formally associated with the party, but it has the greatest potential to see Libertarian candidates elected to local, state and national office in years to come. The Free State Project is a plan to have 20,000 individuals move to a single state within the U.S. Once present and registered to vote, the intent of the Free State Project is to influence local politics in an effort to reduce the size and scope of government at the local, state, and federal levels – essentially to enact libertarian policies.

Inspired by an article published in L. Neil Smith's online magazine *The Libertarian Enterprise* on July 23, 2001, Jason Sorens, a Ph.D. candidate at Yale University at the time, argued that thinly scattered libertarian activism was failing. His conclusion was that it would be necessary for libertarians to geographically concentrate their efforts in order to achieve "liberty in our lifetime." As a result, the Free State Project was founded on September 1, 2001.

When the Free State Project surpassed 5,000 members in August, 2003, a vote was held to choose their target state. The ten candidates were Alaska, Delaware, Idaho, Maine, Montana, New Hampshire, North Dakota, South Dakota, Vermont, and Wyoming. These states were chosen because of their low populations (under 1.5 million), relatively pro-libertarian native cultures, lack of dependence on federal funds, and decent job markets.

The group chose New Hampshire, known for its "Live Free or Die" motto, and absence of a state income tax and state sales tax, as its target. As of 2008, the Free State Project boasted over 8,700 people who have pledged to move to New Hampshire, while nearly 600 have actually moved. In addition, over 250 New Hampshire residents who joined before the state vote are members, raising the count of Free State Project participants in New Hampshire to almost 1000.

Once in New Hampshire, members have pledged to "exert the fullest practical effort toward the creation of a society in which the maximum role of civil government is the protection of life, liberty, and property." This goal would seem to lend itself to the election of libertarian candidates, many of whom may run formally as Libertarians. The aim of Free State Project participants is to work within the political system to reduce the size and scope of government through reductions in taxation and regulation, reforms in state and local law, an end to federal mandates, and a restoration of what they see as constitutional federalism.

Through the Free State Project, the United States may yet witness another wholesale realignment of the political system driven by the doctrinal Libertarian Party. Certainly the Libertarian Party has endured longer than most of the third party trailblazers who have come before, and the effect of the Free State Project on their prognosis is impossible to tell at this time. Furthermore, the shift in the political landscape currently taking place, with greater numbers of voters registering

142

as independents than as either Republicans or Democrats in many jurisdictions, anything is possible.

As has been mentioned previously, the emergence of the Tea Party movement, too, could play into the hands of the Libertarian Party. While the movement remains somewhat disjointed, the unifying theme seems to be distrust of government – the very message that the Libertarian Party is delivering. Whether this means that the Tea Party activists and candidates allow themselves to be absorbed into the Libertarian Party or whether the Libertarian Party finds itself disbanding to re-organize as an official Tea Party is anybody's guess. Nonetheless, the possibility of seeing the United States emerge as a three-party state could ultimately come to pass, as could a realignment not seen since before the Civil War. For anyone reading this book, the mere prospect is exhilarating.

A Threat to Left & Right from the Outside:
Reform Party

Do the right thing

- Ross Perot,
Reform Party Founder and Presidential Candidate

The end of the Cold War caused a fundamental shift in national politics leading into the 1992 elections. With the possible exception of 1968, for the first time since the Great Depression, the economy and domestic policy clearly trumped foreign affairs as the central issue in the campaign. The economy was still feeling the effects of the 1990-91 recession and the economic insecurities of Americans, especially with respect to the consequences of free trade, featured prominently in the campaign. Despite the differences between the major party candidates in 1992, the issue of free trade, which both supported, provided the opening for a unique candidacy in U.S. history and the birth of a new third party – The Reform Party. In 1992, Texas Billionaire Ross Perot ran the most powerful candidacy of a non-major party candidate since Theodore Roosevelt in 1912.

The altered political landscape of 1992 was best summed up by the mantra of the Democratic nominee, then-Governor of Arkansas Bill Clinton, who bluntly stated, "it's the economy, stupid!" However, both Clinton and incumbent president, George H.W. Bush, supported the newly negotiated North American Free Trade Agreement, or NAFTA. To the economically anxious American worker, NAFTA threatened massive job losses to Mexico. During the campaign Perot described NAFTA's potential effect on U.S. jobs as a "giant sucking sound!" The colorful language of the 1992 election was enhanced by the advent of cable television news, which provided non-stop coverage and helped usher in the modern political campaign.

In early 1992 Ross Perot was interviewed on the Larry King Live program on CNN. During the interview, Perot announced that he would run for president if the people would help him secure ballot access in all 50 states. Perot's announcement was dismissed by many. Perot's critics claimed that his personal presence, he was short with pronounced ears and a high-pitched, nasally speaking voice, lacked the charisma and gravitas necessary for a successful presidential candidate. Nonetheless, although relatively unknown outside the business community, Perot had a compelling populist message and self-made image that quickly drew supporters throughout the nation.

Perot's personal story, from successful entrepreneur to the daring commando raid he helped engineer to rescue two employees held captive in Iran, imbued Perot with a can-do problem solver image to which Americans gravitated toward to pull them out of their economic malaise. He used television as a powerful tool to reach voters, giving interviews, producing numerous political ads, and even appearing in lengthy paid infomercials, which featured the candidate, with extensive charts and graphs, explaining the problems facing the nation and his plan to fix them. Perot spoke of "taking back America" and his populist outreach attracted millions.[34] Remarkably, by June Perot was leading Clinton and Bush in the polls, garnering 37 percent support to Bush's 33 and Clinton's 25.

Despite Perot's lead, on July 16 he suspended his campaign. This decision proved fatally damaging, and his various justifications for this decision only furthered the self-inflicted harm. At one point Perot asserted his desire to spare the nation the risk of a deadlocked electoral college, later he accused Republican operatives of threatening to sabotage his daughter's wedding. *Newsweek Magazine* featured Perot on its cover under the headline "QUITTER." Perot's supporters left him in droves, thinking he had betrayed them and the cause for which they were fighting. However, Perot's campaign never fully ended; he maintained campaign

---

[34] This same notion of "taking back America" is the very same socio-political undercurrent being fed into and fed off of by the Tea Party activists that arrived on the scene starting shortly after the 2008 presidential election. Perot's ambiguous success and the Tea Party's as yet unrealized potential clearly evidence a stable element of the contemporary body politic ready to venture into alternative politics for the sake of restoring what they see as failures in the political status quo. The question always remains as to how permanent this undercurrent is, and whether cyclical economics can just as easily quash it as fuel it.

offices throughout the country and continued to work with advisors to craft his political platform.

Some generous observers have suggested that Perot's departure was strategic. Under this theory, Perot merely sought to step outside the process to allow Clinton and Bush to assail each other on the campaign trail while Perot remained untarnished. Feeding this theory is the fact that in August, Perot released his platform in book form during the Republican national convention. Entitled, *United We Stand: How We Can Take Back Our Country*, the manifesto became a national best-seller. Whatever the reason for his departure, on October 1, Ross Perot announced he was returning to the campaign trail.

After resuming his campaign, Perot was dogged by the "quitter" moniker. By the time Perot reemerged as a candidate, Clinton had established himself as the clear front-runner in the campaign. During the presidential debates that year Perot reserved his most scathing attacks for Bush. These attacks further eroded support for Bush, and exit polls found that more of Perot's support came from Republicans than from Democrats. Perot ended up receiving about 19% of the popular vote, a record level of popularity not seen in an independent candidacy since former President Theodore Roosevelt ran on the "Bull Moose" Progressive ticket in 1912. All this despite the confused nature of the Perot campaign.

The results of the 1992 election were extraordinary. Ross Perot captured the third largest share of votes of any other candidate not running on a major party ticket in the history of the United States. Only two other candidates, former presidents both, Theodore Roosevelt, running as a Bull Moose Progressive and Millard Fillmore, running as an American Know-Nothing, and enjoying national name recognition and an established political base have done better. Perot's candidacy had the great potential to emerge as a new, permanent force on the national stage and realign national politics. To look back on this period of

American politics is easy to do with 20/20 hindsight, but the sense was that America's political system was poised for nothing short of revolutionary change.

Some argue that Perot's candidacy already had altered the course of the campaign; after the election of Bill Clinton, many Republicans argued that because Perot drew more support from Republicans than Democrats, his candidacy cost George H.W. Bush the election. Only in Clinton's home state of Arkansas did any candidate win a majority of votes. Ross Perot's votes could, therefore, have ultimately determined the outcome in states representing 529 of the 538 total electoral votes!

Perot continued being politically involved after the election. In November 1993, Perot engaged Vice President Al Gore in a debate over the issue of NAFTA that remains one of the most widely watched political events in U.S. history. Perot formally turned his campaign organization into a lobbying group he called *United We Stand*. *United We Stand* eventually became the vehicle through which Perot and his followers would form the Reform Party.

Following the 1994 midterm elections the Republicans took control of the House of Representatives, largely on the strength of the "Contract With America", which recognized and promised to deal with many of the issues Perot's voters had mobilized to support in 1992. However, failure to enact legislation on two of the major positions of Perot's candidacy, constitutional amendments for term limits and balanced budgets, led to a turning away from the Republican Party and renewed interest in Perot and his organization. Dissatisfied grassroots activists, many of whom supported the Republican take-over of Congress in 1994 and who had made Perot's 1992 candidacy possible, began to band together to found a third party intended to rival the Republicans and Democrats. A drive to get the party on the ballot in all fifty states succeeded, although in a few states, independent minor parties became incorporated as Reform Party-affiliated state organizations.

When the 1996 election season arrived, Perot at first held off from entering the contest for the Reform Party's nomination, calling for others to try for the ticket. The only person who announced such an intention was Dick Lamm, former Governor of Colorado. After the Federal Election Commission ruled that, because Perot had run as an independent in 1992 and not as a candidate for the Reform Party, only Perot and not Lamm would be able to secure federal matching funds for the 1996 campaign, Perot jumped into the campaign to become the Reform Party candidate.[35] Perot's decision to run in 1996 so as not to forfeit these funds led to the beginning of a factional splintering within the movement. The Reform party was barely a year old and was already showing the signs of collapse that have plagued so many third parties in the past. The issue of federal financing would further exacerbate these divisions in the Reform Party going into the 2000 election cycle as well, and forever alter the course of the party's history and fate. Despite the rancor in 1996, eventually Perot was nominated.

Between 1992 and 1996, the Commission on Presidential Debates changed its rules regarding how candidates could qualify to participate in the presidential debates.[36] Perot had previously done very well in the 1992 debates; some polls showed him even winning two out of the three. The CPD's decision was a decisive blow to the campaign when the Commission ruled that he could not participate on the basis of vague and arbitrary criteria. The CPD determined that a candidate was required to have already been endorsed by "a substantial number of major news organizations", with "substantial" being a number to be decided by the Commission

---

[35] No doubt the fact that only Democrats and Republicans sit on the FEC helped determine this decision. Cynics would suggest that the decision itself was not about interpretation of statutes and regulations, but rather the manifestation of the duopoly seeking to deny these funds to a nascent, and very threatening, third party. So would realists.

[36] Again, the Commission on Presidential Debates is governed exclusively by Democrats and Republicans. The changed criteria were another measure that all but guaranteed a continuation of the duopolistic control of visibility in the presidential debates, and therefore the perception, for many, of viability and electability.

on a case-by-case basis. Perot could not have qualified for the debates in 1992 under these rules, and was able to show that various famous US presidents would likewise have been excluded from modern debate by the Commission on Presidential Debates.

Despite legal action by the Perot team, and an 80% majority of Americans supporting his participation in the debates, the Commission refused to budge and Perot was reduced to making his points heard via a series of half-hour "commercials." In the end, Perot captured only 8% of the popular vote. Perot's performance at the polls, however, still ranks him at the top of third-party candidates in the nation's history. More importantly, it surpassed the 5% threshold necessary to again entitle Perot to federal campaign funds, only this time the Reform Party, and not Perot alone, could claim these funds.

By 1997, factional disputes began to emerge within the Reform Party. A small group left the party due to their belief that Perot had rigged the 1996 party primary to defeat Lamm. Perot himself chose to leave the party to its own devices, concentrating on lobbying efforts through United We Stand America. Despite the exit of some Perot supporters and some party members, Perot's departure helped breath new life into the movement. No longer was the party a Perot vanity project, and by the 1998 mid-term elections it looked as though the Reform Party might escape the fate of such personality-dominated parties as the Bull Moose Party.

In 1998, the Reform Party received a boost when former professional wrestler Jesse "the Body" Ventura was elected governor of Minnesota. According to the Women's League of Voters, Reform candidates obtained more votes nationwide in 1998 than did any other third party in America, even without those garnered by Ventura. Counting Ventura's performance, Reformers took in more votes than all other third parties in the United States *combined*, establishing the Reform Party as America's third largest party, and, therefore, largest third party.

This was a particularly impressive feat when one considers that none of Perot's money, influence or organization was involved in any of the candidacies, including Ventura's. The party was operating entirely on its own resources, and had in fact run fewer candidates with less money than the next most-popular party, the Libertarians. No sooner had the Reform Party scored these impressive gains did they return to the fracturing that bedeviled them when Perot jumped into the 1996 race. Shortly after being elected governor, Ventura joined the Independent Party of Minnesota when that group broke from the national Reform Party. He did not seek reelection in 2002.

Due to Perot's performance in 1996, the Reform Party's presidential candidate for the 2000 election was due federal matching funds of $12.5 million. This money made the nomination an attractive target to would-be candidates. After a bitter fight that culminated in two Reform Party conventions being held simultaneously, former Republican Pat Buchanan secured the Reform Party nomination over John Hagelin[37]. Buchanan captured less than half a million votes, or 0.4% of those voting, and the party lost its matching funds for 2004. In 2002, Buchanan returned to the Republican Party. The party had been mortally wounded by this second round of in-fighting over federal funds and lack of leadership. Buchanan's poor showing also cost the party ballot access in nearly every state.

Beyond the internal battles over control of the Reform Party, the 2000 election was a difficult one for all third parties. The controversy over Ralph Nader's role in the outcome of the Florida election cast third parties in a negative light and labeled them spoilers. However, Buchanan's role perhaps had as great or greater of

---

[37] Hagelin, a particle physicist, is a three-time presidential candidate for the Natural Law Party, a party whose positions were based on the Transcendental Meditation teachings of Maharishi Mahesh Yogi. While he did remain on a handful of state Reform Party ballot lines in 2000 (as well as the Independence Party line in New York State) due to the loose affiliation between state parties and the national Reform Party, Hagelin ran as the Natural Law Party candidate in that party's last campaign before disbanding..

an impact as Nader's. In four states won by Gore in 2000, Iowa, New Mexico, Oregon and Wisconsin, Gore won by a margin of less than half a percent of the popular vote. The 31 collective electoral votes of these states are greater than those of Florida. It is entirely possible that but for Buchanan's presence on the ballot in these states, Republican candidate George W. Bush would have captured these states and rendered the Florida election irrelevant to the outcome of the election.[38] Not so much a realignment, but certainly an enormous impact on a highly contentious and divisive election.

By the October 2003 National Reform Party Convention, the party had only begun rebuilding itself. Several former state organizations chose to rejoin the Reform Party. Due to the organizational and financial problems of the party, it opted to support the independent campaign of Ralph Nader as the best option for an independent of any stripe that year. While the endorsement generated publicity for Nader and the Reform Party, the party was only able to provide Nader with seven ballot lines down from the 49 state ballots to which the party had access going into the 2000 election. By the 2008 election, the Reform Party's ballot access had been reduced to a single state – Mississippi.

In the 1992 and 1996 elections, Ross Perot appeared to be on the verge of what no other third party had accomplished in over a century, emerging as a major party. His vote total in 1992, especially, threatened to unravel the two-party system extant since the emergence of the Republican Party in the middle of the 19th century. The Reform Party failed to establish itself as a true national party, however. Too many candidates, over too many election cycles, were fighting over

---

[38] Notwithstanding this electoral math and the very real impact it likely had, the entirety of the narrative about the 2000 presidential election remains, to this day, about Florida. Part of the reason for this single-minded focus depends largely on the fact that too many "what ifs" exist in the analysis of multiple state calculations. The other part, no doubt, is entirely dependent on the ease of targeting the butterfly-ballots and hanging chads of the unquestionably haplessly executed election in Florida that year.

what the party stood for and who would control its destiny.   Factionalism condemned the party to ever-worsening election results.   Additionally, with the departure of Perot, the party quickly succumbed to the fate of all previous third parties that originally coalesce around a personality as their genesis.

Internal fighting and lack of access to the process doomed the party. Nonetheless, the party did play a significant realignment role in American politics. Whether decisive in the outcome, Perot's candidacy certainly aided President Clinton in breaking twelve years of Republican control of the White House.   The Democratic Clinton administration took on the Reform Party's crusade against deficits and even managed to balance the budget and begin paying down the national debt.   Due to the budget reforms of President Clinton, the infamous billboard-sized National Debt clock in New York City began running backwards and was actually switched off for a time.

Following Clinton, the administration of Republican George W. Bush nearly doubled the nation's debt from a little under six trillion dollars to nearly 11 trillion dollars.[39]   After the embrace of deficit and debt reduction by Clinton, the subsequent profligate spending under President Bush may grant the Reform Party a new lease on life or afford it a somewhat delayed realigning impact well beyond its lifespan.   The Republican Party, long considered the party of fiscal responsibility, and the Democratic Party, regularly lambasted as the party of tax-and-spend policies, may see their roles and reputations reversed or merged.   It seems likely, though, that many former Reform Party supporters constitute a significant segment of the Tea Party movement's numbers.   As such, it appears these activists have found a new home, whether within or without the Republican Party; only time will tell.   Eventually, the Reform Party's objectives may be realized, whether through

---

[39] With the onset of the financial crisis in 2008 and the Recession it engendered, this figure continues to rise. With the reemergence of deficits so too have the populist deficit fighters. The story of third parties also seems ideally situated for its next chapter.

major party cooption or embrace by a future third party. Nonetheless, it does not appear that there will be a Reform Party around to see it.

Red, White & Green:

The Green Party

"The Green Party is no longer the alternative,
the Green Party is the imperative."

- Rosa Clemente,
2008 Green Party Vice-Presidential Candidate

While it is impossible to identify any particular date or event that launched political environmentalism in the United States, a few historic landmarks help chronicle what would eventually coalesced into the Green Party in the United States. In the modern age, the most significant of these milestones occurred on April 22, 1970. On that date, United States Senator Gaylord Nelson helped to organize the first ever Earth Day, which for all intents and purposes officially launched political environmental activism in the United States. Today, despite significant political setbacks, the Green Party carries the banner of political environmentalism.

Like the Progressive Bull Moose Party, the Green Party is essentially a broad-based doctrinal party, seeking systemic changes in U.S. politics geared toward pro-environmental policies. Nonetheless, due to the events of the 2000 presidential election, the Green Party has played a realignment role in national politics as well.[40] This realignment cut two ways – the presence of Green Party Candidate Ralph Nader in that election altered the outcome of that contest in historically predictive ways; but due to the result of the 2000 election, Nader and the Green Party almost single-handedly crippled the aspirations of third parties and their candidates in contemporary American politics.[41]

America has always had a love affair with its natural splendor. From its earliest days the United States has also had a unique brand of environmentalism, borne of the same sense of exceptionalism that has marked nearly every other aspect of the American story. Figures such as Henry David Thoreau and John Muir were early proponents of preserving the natural gifts of the United States. After living close to nature for over two years in a cabin near Walden Pond in Concord

---

[40] The Green Party's role in the 2000 presidential has also likely condemned it to a lengthy, if not permanent, place as *persona non grata* amongst many voters otherwise inclined to support the party.
[41] This reality may explain why, primary elections aside, the Tea Party activists have largely chosen to remain within the Republican Party if not cleave to the Republican establishment itself.

Massachusetts, Thoreau published *Walden* in 1854 to chronicle his experiences and arguing that people should become more intimately connected to the natural world. Muir spent time in the Western United States studying ecology and geology, and his activism help push Congress to establish the Yosemite and Sequoia National Parks in 1890.

The first efforts to protect nature in America, and the first such effort by any government anywhere, came under President Andrew Jackson when he set aside land in 1832 around Hot Springs, Arkansas. This act was followed by President Lincoln's grant of the Yosemite Valley and the Mariposa Grove of Giant Sequoias to the State of California. In signing the Congressional act ceding these lands, Lincoln stated that California "shall accept this grant upon the express conditions that the premises shall be held for public use, resort, and recreation; shall be inalienable for all time." The world's first truly public national park was likewise formed in the United States; in 1872, Yellowstone National Park was created.

In 1916, President Wilson signed the National Park Service Organic Act to establish the National Park Service as the overseer of the growing patchwork of national parks in the United States. The National Park Service consolidated the national parks throughout the United States, but these largely rural and western preserves did little to address the damage and encroachment of industrialization. The social and political activism of the 1960s transformed this form of environmentalism from grand gestures by the federal government to a popular movement.

In 1965 two events brought environmental activism into the national spotlight. First, a group of local activists won a landmark legal decision against Consolidated Edison, the New York-based energy goliath. ConEd had never lost a challenge made to curtail its efforts to expand its energy infrastructure in New York State, and the lawsuit set the precedent for legal environmental rights. That same

157

year, the book *Silent Spring* sounded the alarm of the use of DDT and its affect on the environment, specifically its role as a carcinogen and its detrimental effect on bird populations. The national conscience was stirred and now had tools with which to fight.

At the end of the decade, U.S. Senator Gaylord Nelson of Wisconsin proposed the first nationwide environmental protest to thrust the environment onto the national agenda. Five months before the first Earth Day, as it was termed, *The New York Times* carried a lengthy article reporting on the growing environmental movement in the United States:

> Rising concern about the environmental crisis is sweeping the nation's campuses with an intensity that may be on its way to eclipsing student discontent over the war in Vietnam ... a national day of observance of environmental problems ... is being planned for next spring ... when a nationwide environmental 'teach-in' ... coordinated from the office of Senator Gaylord Nelson is planned....

20 million people, nearly 10% of the U.S. population at that time, participated in coast-to-coast rallies, protests and educational events. Political environmentalism had arrived.

The 1960s and 1970s saw a rash of environmental legislation, including the creation of the U.S. Environmental Protection Agency. However, after this initial burst of grassroots and governmental activism, environmental activism stalled. No significant events or progress in the immediate aftermath of this initial burst of activity can be pointed to.

In 1984 a group called the Green Committees of Correspondence was formed intent on organizing environmental groups at the local level with the ultimate goal of forming a national Green political organization in the United States. After an internal split and restructuring, the Greens/Green Party USA

158

became the successor political organization to the Committees. The Greens/Green Party USA never fully embraced electoral politics and preferred to emphasize local, grassroots efforts. In fact, the Greens/Green Party USA no longer enjoys Federal Election Commission status as a political party. Nonetheless, the interest existed in forming a Green political party.

At the time of the decline of the Greens/Green Party USA, a collection of state-based Green Parties formed as the Association of Autonomous State Green Parties. Recognizing that political realities required state-based political organization and state-by-state ballot access, a meeting was held to have state Green Parties nominate a single candidate for the 1996 presidential election. That candidate was Ralph Nader.

Ralph Nader was not formally nominated by the Green Party. Instead, he appeared on ballots in 22 states as an independent candidate or as a candidate of that state's Green Party. With the high profile inclusion of third party candidate Ross Perot, and Nader's refusal to campaign or raise money, little attention was paid to this "fourth" (or "fifth") third party candidacy and Nader garnered approximately seven-tenths of one percent of the popular vote. However, Nader did substantially better than Libertarian Party candidate Harry Brown who appeared on ballots in all 50 states and the District of Columbia.

In the lead up to the 2000 presidential election, the Association of Autonomous State Green Parties adopted the name Green Party of the United States. Today the Green Party of the United States is the party to which people refer when they talk about the Green Party in the United States. The Green Party again nominated Ralph Nader for president, and Nader decided to campaign vigorously against what he viewed as a two-party duopoly dominated by corporate interests. Nader firmly believed there was essentially no difference between the

Republican and Democratic Parties or their candidates, and so did many of his supporters. Then came the 2000 election and its aftermath.

In the 2000 presidential election Ralph Nader and the Green Party appeared on the ballot in 44 states, and captured nearly 2.7% of the popular vote. It was not the campaign that mattered, it was the election – particularly in the State of Florida. Florida's election proved decisive for the overall election outcome,[42] and the profound realignment that took place in its wake.

In the closing hours of voting on election day many states revealed extremely close results between the Republican and Democratic candidates. However it was the State of Florida that would decide the winner of the election. As the electoral vote results were being tallied, Republican candidate George W. Bush had total of 246 electoral votes, while Democratic candidate Al Gore had won 255 votes. New Mexico and Oregon, still too close to call, would not decide the election as neither had sufficient electoral votes even if won by a single candidate. It was Florida's 25 electoral votes that would decide the next president of the United State.

The history of what happened next is well known. A drawn out recount effort and legal battles were waged by the Republican and Democratic campaigns to secure Florida's electoral votes and, thus, the presidency. In Florida, Nader won nearly 100,000 votes; ultimately Bush carried the state by 537 votes. Though each third party candidate in the race received more votes than the final vote count difference between Bush and Gore, it was Nader's campaign that many believe cost Gore the election.

National polling showed that Nader supporters preferred Gore over Bush by substantial margins. In some studies, 46% of Nader voters nation-wide would have picked Gore in a two-way race, 23% would have chosen Bush, and over 30%

---

[42] Electoral math regarding Buchanan's Reform Party candidacy notwithstanding.

would not have voted for either. Extrapolating from these national figures, it is clear that Gore might well have enjoyed a net gain of over 20,000 votes had Nader not run in Florida, turning a protracted vote recount battle into a decisive win for Gore. The effect of the Florida vote and the 2000 election cannot be overstated for its impact on national and third party politics.

For one, in an unprecedented move, the U.S. Supreme Court became the final arbiter of the election dispute,[43] seemingly in violation of the U.S. Constitution, which leaves election dispute resolution to the House of Representatives.[44] In his dissent from the majority decision that effectively handed the presidency to Bush, Justice John Paul Stevens declared that, "[a]lthough we may never know with complete certainty the identity of the winner of this year's presidential election, the identity of the loser is perfectly clear. It is the nation's confidence in the judge as an impartial guardian of the rule of law."

With the outcome of the election final, the real impact of Nader's Green Party candidacy became clear. Though the Green Party is a staunch advocate of global environmental leadership by the United States, it would appear their campaign handed the election to diametrically opposed ideologues. While Nader argued that there was no difference between the Republican and Democratic candidates running for office in 2000, the histories of these two candidates on the doctrinal issue of import to the Green Party – the environment – could not be more dissimilar.

Al Gore is a life-long environmentalist. He credits his mother's reading of *Silent Spring* while he was in high school and the launch of Earth Day at the time of his college graduation as formative moments in his education and impression of

---

[43] *Bush v. Gore* 531 U.S. 98; 121 S. Ct. 525; 148 L. Ed. 2d (2000)

[44] This claim and the refutations made against it are sufficient to form the basis of numerous books and articles. Many fine works advocating both sides of this question have been written and, as such, the matter is best left to those authors and the reader.

environmental issues. In 1992, Gore published the book *Earth in the Balance: Ecology and the Human Spirit,* and in 1997 Gore signed the Kyoto Protocol, which sought binding reductions in greenhouse gas emissions. In 2007, Gore received the Nobel Peace Prize for his pro-environmental activism.

George W. Bush, on the other hand, is a former oil company executive who was governor from Texas, one of America's pre-eminent fossil-fuel producing states. Bush questioned the science behind global climate change and, once in office, President Bush withdrew U.S. support for the Kyoto Protocol. For Green Party supporters concerned with the environment as their political priority, the contrast could not be starker.

For a Green Party candidate to be accused of being the cause of Bush's victory over Gore is devastating. Democrats who chose Nader over Gore due to their doctrinal passions for the environment above all else were left believing they had handed the presidency to the exact opposite of what they hoped for when they cast their votes. Independents, and those who might not have otherwise voted, likewise found themselves with a president as far from the Green Party platform as is imaginable. The reservations and regrets over voting for Nader and the Green Party in 2000 resonate to this day.

In 2004 Nader again ran for president, but the Green Party selected David Cobb as its candidate. Ballot access for the Green Party shrank from 43 states in 2000 to 25 in the 2004 election. Though Ralph Nader still came in third in the 2004 election, his popular vote plummetted below 500,000 and most likely benefited from greater ballot access and name recognition than Cobb's Green Party candidacy. Cobb received less than 120,000 votes and the Green Party was, quite literally, decimated.

While environmental politics still hold great appeal for many American voters, it appears that, for the time being, the Green Party has suffered the fate of many past doctrinal parties. In the 2008 presidential campaign, the Democratic candidate Barak Obama and Democratic leaders in Congress advocated aggressive, pro-environmental policies. The 2008 Green Party candidate, former representative Cynthia McKinney barely managed to register amongst the electorate.[45] In addition to this classic doctrinal party fate, the Green Party is unique in its realignment role, both realigning national politics and third party politics. Rarely has a third party has such effect on an election, the dynamic between the major parties, their own fate, and the fate of current and as-yet-unformed third parties for the foreseeable future.

In 2000, Al Gore was the vice president of a popular President in a time of peace and prosperity. Though many argue that Gore ran a lackluster campaign in 2000, losing his home state and that of the incumbent president, most liberals, progressives and, especially, environmentalists, still attribute his loss to Florida, the Green Party and Ralph Nader. The realigning quality of the Green Party candidacy in 2000 was to shift the White House from Democratic to Republican hands. Immediately thereafter, with a Republican majority in both houses of congress, President Bush began to implement an aggressive conservative agenda.

Most importantly in the story of the Green Party is the fact that the party, more than any other party in any other election, has cast great doubt on the wisdom of voting for a third party. For the first time in American history, the greatest consequence of a third party candidacy may be as a realignment in third party politics rather than in the politics of the major parties. Due to the complexities of the U.S. presidential election system, many Green Party supporters

---

[45] This lack of attention to McKinney's Green Party candidacy is probably for the best when considering the long-term viability of the Green Party in its present incarnation. McKinney has been widely ridiculed and criticized for her extreme positions and embrace of conspiracy theory – certainly not the best persona in which to wrap a nascent political movement seeking to restore its credibility after Nader and the 2000 election.

in traditional "safe states" may no longer feel they can safely vote for the candidate of their choice, or send a signal to the major parties for fear of handing the election to their least desired candidate. Despite its relevance to any given state's election, many will use Nader's Green Party candidacy to buttress the "spoiler" candidacy or wasted vote argument for years to come. With their doctrinal positions being partly adopted by the Democratic Party and suffering a self-inflicted anti-third party realignment, the Green Party may find future elections rather uninviting.

Being Left Right Out:

The Barriers to Third Parties

the best test of truth is the power of the thought to get itself accepted in the competition of the market ... That at any rate is the theory of our Constitution.

– United States Supreme Court Justice Oliver Wendell Holmes

The sheer enormity of the United States and its vast diversity – ethnic, religious, and economic – contains all the elements for a vibrant multiparty system. Indeed, many much smaller nations with relatively homogenous populations swarm with a multitude of parties that is incredulous to the American observer. Nonetheless, America has, for the most part, retained its two-party system in the face of dramatic change in its social, economic and political makeup throughout its history.

The cause of this entrenched duoply is not lack of interest in a political alternative. Public opinion has consistently shown widespread support for a third party – both opinion polls and election results bear that out. However, historic, systemic, and social factors provide substantial impediment to the emergence of a national third party.

Revolutionary America was a far different place than the United States of today. At its founding, America's political class was a mainly white, male, protestant one. Divisions between urban and rural interests, or geographic sectionalism were inherently dualistic. In fact, the central issue of the day, the adoption and ratification of the U.S. Constitution, was a strictly yes-no proposition.

As the nation grew in size and diversity, and slowly expanded suffrage to all its citizens, the increasing socio-political complexity of the country changed its politics, but not the two-party system. On the contrary, American diversity has consistently seen the political dichotomy reinforced rather than destroyed by change. Even the collapse of the Whigs and the era of dynamic third party experimentation marked by the Anti-Masonic Party, the Know Nothings, and others only seemed to mark the transition into a new duopoly of Republicans and Democrats, which endures to the present day. In times of political realignment major issues formed the nexus of political alliance along the two-party division rather than caused a rupture of the same; doctrinal parties have failed to make

166

their causes the impetus of a lasting, popular political movement separate from the major parties.

The history of third parties in the United States is replete with examples of political movements being absorbed into the major parties. The Liberty and Free Soil Parties caused a permanent realignment in the form of the emergence of the Republican Party. The Populist Party's doctrines became core elements of the Democratic Party in later years. Additionally, parties such as the Prohibition Party have virtually ceased to exist as their doctrinal foundation lost appeal and vanished from the American political forum.

While extremism is extant in American society, no group of fanatics is so numerous that it poses a real threat to the major parties. Communists, racists, theologists and other extremists either find themselves isolated in marginal political movements or are forced to attempt to compete for influence within either of the major parties. Ultimately the rejection of extremism and the inclusion of less moderate factions within the major parties has resulted in broad center-right or center-left coalitions that make the Republicans and Democrats competitive for the vote of the vast majority of Americans. The major parties are further aided, and third parties further frustrated, by the system in which these grand coalitions compete.

The American executive is determined through a separate, national election[46] and not one drawn from the ranks of the legislative branch as is done in most parliamentary systems. This electoral dynamic incentivizes the formation of broad political coalitions capable of capturing the White House. The presidential election further encourages broad political alliances due to the first-past-the post system used in American elections.

---

[46] Or, rather, a broad, usually winner-take-all, state-by-state election that actually further diminishes the competitiveness of third parties.

167

In a first-past-the post, or plurality-based, election system, a single winner is chosen in a given election by having more votes than any other individual candidate; there is no requirement that the winner gain an absolute majority of votes. Without the use of proportional voting as utilized in many other countries, there is no prize for second or third place. The result of the plurality system in place in the United States is that even in elections where third parties have done extremely well they are not able to translate that success into political clout unless they capture seats in the Congress. However, the use of single-district voting for seats in the Congress makes third party success in the legislature as difficult as that in the executive branch of government

Unlike many systems found around the world, in which candidates stand as part of party lists in proportional voting, each election in the United States runs as a single representative from a single election district. Therefore, a third party that captures 20 percent of the vote in every congressional district will not find itself with one-fifth of the seats in Congress or a state legislature, instead they will have none. Alternatively, a party that succeeds in garnering even a plurality – not even a majority – in every election district would command 100% of all legislative seats!

Single member districts in a first-past-the-post system, though, are not themselves a decisive obstacle to third parties. However, even when third parties are victorious in individual election districts, these victories have not guaranteed long-term success. The real institutional barrier to third parties has always been the Electoral College.

Under the often misunderstood system of the Electoral College, an absolute majority of electoral votes is required to elect a president. However, all but a few states in American history have allocated their electoral votes on a winner-take-all basis. Therefore, a simple plurality in a state affords the winning candidate all of the state's electoral votes. Again, a strong performance by a third party candidate would result in few if any electoral votes. Candidates with strong regional appeal have managed to secure the electoral votes of a few states, but not enough to seriously stand a chance of winning the presidency.

Failure to win sufficient electoral votes does not leave third party candidates without the possibility of having a great impact on elections. Paradoxically, this ability to influence election outcomes has rendered third parties less, not more, appealing during presidential campaigns, especially in recent years. Given the fact that third party candidates stand little chance of winning, many voters feel that casting a vote for a third party is a wasted vote. The possibility of a voter's least favorite candidate winning by splitting the vote of like-minded voters has given rise to the notion of the spoiler effect. The greatest example of this fear is the marked drop-off in third party support following the 2000 election.[47] The notion of the wasted vote and the spoiler effect provide tremendous disincentive to vote for third party candidates. Both these phenomena would remain powerful obstacles to third party success even absent the structural barriers currently working against third parties.

The wasted vote theory is a simple one. Basically, the notion is that if a third party candidate has no chance of winning, voting for the third party is a waste. The problem with this theory is that if collectively acted upon it becomes a self-fulfilling prophecy. If everyone believes the third party candidate cannot win, and therefore does not vote for the candidate, the candidate stands no chance of winning. In reality, if a candidate appears on the ballot in enough states to achieve a majority in the Electoral College the candidate does, in fact, have a chance of winning the presidency. However, despite the mathematical ability of any given

---

[47] It cannot be stated often enough: the vast majority of Nader voters in 2000 did not see George W. Bush as their second choice, or even a palatable option in any way, shape, or form.

third party candidate to succeed, many voters view voting for a third party candidate to be a wasted vote nonetheless. This belief is based upon a very real concern, namely that voting for one's candidate of choice could result in the victory of a voter's least favorite option.

For example, in a three-way race between a center-right, a center-left and a far-left candidate, voting for the far-left candidate could help the center-right candidate achieve a plurality and thus win the election. Clearly a voter adhering to a doctrinal-based political philosophy by voting for the far-left third party candidate does not desire the election of a center-right candidate. To avoid such an outcome, many voters will not act in such a doctrinaire fashion, and will rather choose what they view as the lesser-of-two-evils, or, in this example, the center-left candidate. It is here that the wasted vote theory dovetails with the notion of the spoiler effect.

Third parties suffer from this paradox – if everyone believes they cannot win nobody will vote for them and they have no chance of winning, but if a sufficiently large minority of voters do cast their vote for the third party candidate of their choice, they run the risk of handing the election to a candidate with diametrically opposed positions to the values of the voters supporting the third party candidate. In these circumstances the few voters sufficiently ardent in their beliefs stand the greatest chance of handing the election to the candidate with whom they disagree to the greatest extent. The wasted vote theory, therefore, lays the groundwork for the spoiler effect.

Despite protests to the contrary, many of Ralph Nader's supporters in 2000 were natural Democratic voters who likely would have handed Florida's electoral votes, and thus the presidency, to Al Gore. George W. Bush's victory in that election, and his subsequent hard-right governing style, forced many voters to rethink their support of Nader again in 2004. Between 2000 and 2004, Nader's vote count fell from nearly 2.9 million to under 500,000. This drop is the direct result of many voters believing that Nader played a spoiler role in 2000 and cost Gore the election, thus handing the White House to Bush. Given a choice between Nader, Gore, and Bush, few, if any, Nader supporters would have opted for Bush as their second choice.

Nader and the 2000 election have essentially become the case study against third party support. It is difficult to see the conditions in which a third party will emerge in the next few election cycles that will repair or overcome the impression left by Nader.[48] The two elements that could help in this effort, however, return us to questions of the systemic obstacles to third parties.

Before any talk of wasted votes and spoiler affects, however, third party candidates must first actually appear on the ballot. The American federal system creates a confusing tangle of state ballot access laws with which each aspiring third party must contend. Even were each state to establish low thresholds to appear on a ballot, the myriad systems in place create a challenge to third parties requiring teams of election lawyers and volunteers. The standards for ballot access are not set uniformly low, however. In many cases parties and candidates must obtain a significant number of signatures to appear on the ballot, in other cases a formula is used based on voter turnout in prior elections. In either case the major parties

---

[48] In fact, the threat of Sarah Palin or some other extreme conservative candidate as a very real possibility to run for and win the Republican nomination could further depress the enthusiasm of otherwise likely third party voters. On the one hand the degree to which these candidates harbor and articulate extreme populist views could lend itself to keeping many potential right-wing third party voters within the Republican Party. On the other hand, the risk of splitting the liberal vote and handing the election to one of these potential candidates will likely serve to ensure that potential left-wing third party voters will cast their votes for incumbent president Barack Obama. With the rise in populist outrage against the state of the economy and the seeming inability of Washington to fix the problems facing the nation, the stars appear aligned for another strong third party showing; the fear of many of a repeat of 2000 and a president Palin would tend to contradict this prediction. For third parties, the 2012 presidential election could prove to be the best of times and the worst of times. Should a strong third party emerge on the left that ultimately is viewed as handing the election to the Republican Party, leftist third parties may virtually disappear from the American landscape for generations. Alternatively, if a conservative third party is viewed as costing the GOP their chance to render President Obama a one term president, their hopes may be dashed for years to come.

often automatically or easily qualify to appear on state ballots. Again, though, once a third party gets its candidate on the ballot in one or more states, first-past-the-post voting and the Electoral College remain tremendous obstacles.

It is clear that plurality first-past-the-post voting and the Electoral College present challenges even when a popular third party candidate, such as Theodore Roosevelt or Ross Perot is already making a strong run for the presidency. These barriers are entrenched in our constitution or state laws on electoral vote allocation and are therefore extremely difficult to alter. Two other impediments to third parties, public campaign finance and the Commission on Presidential Debates, however, are easily revised, and would do much to open the door to third parties and their candidates.

In the early 20th century, President Theodore Roosevelt championed campaign finance reform to limit the influence of corporations on the political process. In response, Congress enacted the Tillman Act, which was followed by several other statutes over the ensuing 60 years. The cumulative effect of these measures was to limit the disproportionate influence of wealthy individuals and special interest groups on the outcome of federal elections and mandate financial disclosure of campaign finances.

In 1971, the U.S. Congress passed the Federal Election Campaign Act. Most notable amongst its provisions, as they affect third parties, is the establishment of public funding for presidential campaigns. FECA was amended by the Bipartisan Campaign Reform Act, otherwise known as McCain-Feingold after its authors.[49]

At the federal level, public funding is limited to subsidies for presidential candidates. To receive subsidies in the primary, candidates must qualify by

---

[49] As has been noted, this legislative measure, and its intent, has been largely gutted by the U.S. Supreme Court in it *Citizens United* ruling.

privately raising $5000 each in at least 20 states. For qualified candidates, the government provides a dollar for dollar "match" from the government for each contribution to the campaign, up to a limit of $250 per contribution. In return, the candidate agrees to limit his or her spending according to a statutory formula. Clearly, nascent third parties find it difficult to establish nationwide networks of campaign offices without first having substantial financial resources, thus creating a difficult catch-22 for these campaigns.

From the inception of this program in 1976, through 1992, almost all candidates who could qualify for matching funds in primary elections accepted them, and thus the limits on overall financial resources in the campaign. However, in 1996 Republican Steve Forbes opted out of the program and privately funded the majority of his campaign. In 2000, Forbes and George W. Bush, opted out. In 2004, Bush and Democrats John Kerry and Howard Dean chose not to take matching funds in the primary. In 2008, Democrats Hillary Clinton and Barack Obama, and Republicans Rudy Giuliani, Mitt Romney and Ron Paul decided not to take matching funds. By refusing matching funds, these candidates are free to spend as much money as they can raise privately. Thus has begun the slow erosion of the public financing system for primary candidates. As major party candidates break free from the restraints imposed by public financing, third party candidates are left further and further behind.

In addition to primary matching funds, the federal government subsidizes the presidential nominating conventions of the major parties. As these conventions have become spectacularly choreographed media events, which often produce a "bump" in polling for the nominees, the value of the convention financing cannot be overstated. By limiting the subsidies to the Democratic and Republican Parties, the U.S. campaign finance laws all but guarantee the perpetuation of the major parties *ad infinitum*.

Following their nominations, the candidates are then offered the opportunity to accept government funds for the general election. If they accept the government funds, they agree not to raise or spend private funds or to spend more than $50,000 of their personal resources. No major party had turned down government funds for the general election since the program was launched in 1976, until Democratic Barack Obama did so in 2008. Having raised funds far in excess of the sums to which he would have been entitled under the public financing regime, and ultimately going on to win the presidency, President Obama may have driven the final nail in public financing's coffin.

Third party candidates are also eligible for public funding during the general election. However, another catch-22 presents itself in the formula used by the Federal Election Commission. A third party candidate is defined by the FEC as the nominee of a party whose candidate receives between 5 and 25 percent of the total popular vote in the preceding Presidential election. Therefore, the third party must have already performed well in a prior election before they are afforded the resources with which to reasonably be expected to do so.

The amount of public funding to which a third party candidate is entitled is based on the ratio of the party's popular vote in the preceding Presidential election to the average popular vote of the two major party candidates in that election. Though seemingly complex, the formula used is fairly simple. To enter the game a candidate must poll five percent or more of the popular vote to qualify for public financing in the next election. The amount of monies received is based on how well the candidate performs beyond the five percent threshold.

Five percent is not a wholly unreasonable figure. Though obviously arbitrary, it prevents the use of public funds for any and all fringe groups that form themselves into a political party. Furthermore, the five percent figure creates a wholly different campaign strategy for third parties hoping for enduring success.

Rather than compete nationally, some third party candidates have limited their most fervent campaigning to "safe states" – states in which the success of the Republican or Democratic Party candidate is not in doubt – in order to garner the five percent of the vote needed for public funding four years later. Clearly a voter in a "swing state" – those where the outcome of the election cannot normally be predicted with any certainty at the start of the campaign - would be reluctant or even loath to cast a vote for a third party candidate if it was believed they would help hand the election to their least desired candidate. The goal for third parties in this context is not to win any electoral votes, but rather merely to surpass the five percent mark – in essence to live to fight another day.

While many of the significant third parties in American history would not have qualified for public financing under this regime, the vast majority would have. Of course changing the public financing law could be achieved fairly easily. Congress could lower, or raise, the threshold simply by passing a law. No constitutional amendment, as would be needed to alter the Electoral College, or coordinated state action, as would be required to make an impact on the first-past-the-post electoral vote allocation, is involved. The true problem with the five percent threshold for public financing is the way it relates to media access, principally through the presidential debates.

Starting in the 1988 election, presidential debates have been produced and directed by the Commission on Presidential Debates. As a non-profit 501(c)(3) entity, the CPD receives funding from foundations and corporations that effectively sponsor the debates. While nominally non-partisan, the CPD was established in 1987 by Frank Fahrenkopf, a former head of the Republican National Committee, and Paul Kirk, a former head of the Democratic National Committee. At a press conference announcing the commission's creation, Fahrenkopf announced that the commission was unlikely to include third party candidates in the debates, and Kirk stated he personally believed they should be excluded from the debates.

Prior to the formation of the CPD, the League of Women Voters sponsored the presidential debates in 1976, 1980 and 1984. However, in the face of actions undertaken by the campaigns of Republican George H.W. Bush and Democrat Michael Dukakis, the League withdrew, issuing a statement that declared:

> *The League of Women Voters is withdrawing sponsorship of the presidential debates ... because the demands of the two campaign organizations would perpetrate a fraud on the American voter. It has become clear to us that the candidates' organizations aim to add debates to their list of campaign-trail charades devoid of substance, spontaneity and answers to tough questions. The League has no intention of becoming an accessory to the hoodwinking of the American public.*

The League was responding to a secret agreement made between the Bush and Dukakis campaigns that sought to limit debate participation to the major party candidates and select the individuals allowed to moderate the debates and ask questions of the candidates. Into this vacuum came the CPD.

The CPD stipulates that candidates must enjoy 15 percent support amongst the electorate as evidenced by national polling. While Ross Perot was invited to take part in the 1992 debates, and received public funding in 1996, he was excluded from the 1996 debates because he did not attain 15 percent support in national polls during the 1996 campaign. Again Perot polled over five percent and guaranteed the Reform Party public funding in 2000. In the 2000 election, Reform Party candidate Patrick Buchanan, who inherited the public financing earned by Perot, was excluded from the presidential debates. In effect, the American electorate was not able to see what it as paying for. Logic and fairness demand that the five percent threshold for public financing also be applied to invitations to participate in presidential debates.

The role of presidential debates is as important as any event in presidential elections. Without a presence in the debates, it is hard to legitimize a third party and its presidential candidate. Again, the stigma of the wasted vote attaches to non-participants. The duopolistic control of the CPD and the disconnect between the five percent requirement for public financing and the 15 percent polling threshold for debate participation is easily remedied.

A truly independent commission could be established to organize presidential debates. These debates could mandate that all publicly financed candidates be invited to participate. The risk of cacophonous debates would be nonexistent as only a single third party candidate would have qualified in any election since 1992. In contrast, many primary debates feature over a half-dozen candidates vying for their party's nomination. These candidates are permitted to participate in these debates based on internal party rules. There are no rules for presidential debates, rather an abrogation of this important responsibility to the whim of the two major parties at the exclusion of all others.

Each barrier to third parties plays a role to prevent or even prohibit third parties from emerging as major fixtures in the U.S. political landscape. These roles vary in their individual impact, but taken collectively they form an overwhelming obstacle to third party aspirations. Changing even one, such as presidential debate participation, could have a potentially cascading effect on the system. For instance, should a third party's candidates appear in repeated presidential debates, the legitimacy of the parties and their candidates would strengthen as they would likely begin to be seen as a viable alternative to the Democratic and Republican candidates.[50]   With a visible national presence represented by a presidential candidate, the notion of a wasted vote would abate; the effect on local and state elections is hard to predict, but third party candidates sharing the ballot with a candidate included in the presidential debates would also presumably translate into greater success at the polls.

Whatever the changes made, the structural and psychological ones will probably move in tandem. One proposal advanced is for instant-runoff-voting. In this system, voters can rank their choices. If no candidate achieves an absolute majority of votes, the votes for all but the candidates with the two highest vote counts are shifted to their second choice (or third if the second choice is likewise eliminated). In this manner, a candidate who voted for Buchanan in 2000 would probably have seen their vote shifted to Bush, and a Nader voter would likely have been added to Gore. Such candidates would no longer risk playing a spoiler role.

In a nation as diverse as the United States, with its myriad cultures, languages, religions and races, it is hard to conceive of the dearth of political parties. Many Americans enjoy hundreds of television channels but often find themselves with but two candidates to choose from when they enter the voting booth. Changing the system to permit a flourishing in the political marketplace of ideas will not be easy, and there are many strong arguments in favor of a two-party system as it currently stands in the United States. Nonetheless, history demonstrates that the American people often desire, even yearn for, greater political choice.

---

[50] This possibility is not mere assumption or conjecture. Following his appearance in the 1992 presidential debates, Ross Perot's appeal amongst voters rose from under 10 percent to the point that he received slightly less than 20 percent of votes cast that year.

Conclusion

The end of this book, but not third party history ...

While most third parties do not share any universal theme or platform they all have one thing in common. Third parties in the United States are the vehicles for the unheard voices that demand to be heard. In its greatest manifestation this has meant the call for freedom and justice seen in the Liberty, Free Soil, and eventually the Republican Party in the nineteenth century. But, so too, in their time, have the Anti-Masonic, Prohibition and Libertarian Parties, and the others chronicled herein, been the means by which these voices have come together to call for change.

The timing of the emergence of a third party and its trajectory is wholly unknowable. From the very beginning of third party history, random events, such as the Morgan Affair, have had unpredictable ramifications. Economic events, often panics, recessions and depressions, can give rise to a powerful political movement that was theretofore unknown. Other times, such as in The Great Depression, no such thing happens at all.

The seeming consistency throughout this work has been the apparent failure of the third parties featured, mitigated only by ephemeral political success and occasionally more far-reaching policy achievements. However, what these third parties share is their indispensability to American history.

The Democratic and Republican parties, while dominant now for over 150 years, have seen their fortunes often dictated by third parties. While the emergence of a third party often presaged trouble for the more similar major party, the eventual adoption of policy positions into the platform of a major party could be the catalyst to bring it back into power. As such, not only are third parties enduring features of American political history, they are indispensible to how that history has unfolded.

This is the point. Every party featured in this book has enjoyed great success, though a success measured not in poll results but in impact. Without this success, these parties would not have been selected from amongst the countless movements that have appeared throughout U.S. history. Whether they reformed the political process, American society, or a particular major party – and sometimes both major parties simultaneously – the legacy of each of these parties is still with us today. The doctrines that prove too narrow for general electoral success become planks in broader, major party platforms. The realigning consequences of third party involvement in the political process sets America's major parties, politics and society off in new directions that are the very thing we call American history.

As the book demonstrates, third parties are here to stay. Rarely has a decade passed whereby one third party or another was not impacting the political process. This fact matters because the possibility of one emerging at any time must be taken seriously by the major parties, and so even the absence of a third party can influence decision making by the major parties and elected officials. Today, numerous articles are being written about the probability and viability of a centrist third party emerging in force in the next election cycle or two. Alternatively or simultaneously, dissatisfaction with President Obama could invite a primary challenge, or a swing in support to a left-leaning third party.[51] If Republican leadership does not tread carefully, the Tea Party activists within the party could very easily become the Tea Party formally, wholly without the major party.[52]

Just as important to recognizing the permanence of third parties is appreciating the consistency with which third parties have actually enjoyed a degree of electoral success. Failure to grasp this fact, regardless of how frequent a third party candidate may or may not get elected, capture Electoral College votes, or

---

[51] Though, as has been noted, the likelihood of this threat coming from the Green Party is slim given the damage to the brand engendered by the 2000 election.

[52] This possibility would make for some interesting politics as a potential stand-alone Tea Party would emerge already equipped with the benefit and power of incumbency.

affect the outcome of a particular vote, is done at the major parties' peril; they must plan for these eventualities to inoculate against it or craft alternative campaign strategies for success. In the case of amateur and professional historians alike, a lack of understanding of how effective and impactful third party candidates can be can mean, at best, an incomplete education; at worst it can mean ineffective or counterproductive civic participation.

As was mentioned at the outset of this book, third parties provide exceptional expository value to understanding contemporary American society during the life of the parties. Due in part to their ephemeral nature, third parties, more so than the major parties, help to serve as snapshots of the pressing forces at work in the United States during its dynamic history. After all, how many people could know that before the Cold War-era Red Scare, there was the Masonic Scare if not for the Anti-Masonic Party? Without the Greenback Party, who today would know of the fraught struggle over specie that took place over several decades in the post-Civil War era? Third parties isolate these pressing social phenomena and allow us to accurately gauge their appeal and impact.

As the United States is the most powerful country on Earth, and will be for the foreseeable future, understanding its politics is crucial to understanding one of the most powerful forces in contemporary global events. Understanding U.S. politics requires understanding its vibrant and varied society. This understanding is enhanced and made whole by understanding America's third parties.

Afterword

When I began to write this book the simple mission was to provide a product that did not exist. The book itself finds its origins in a book store visit when the author went to find, well, this book. Realizing that the only way to know all I wanted to know would require the reading of countless other works, that is exactly what I set out to do. Somewhere along the way I decided to provide the missing product for which I was initially searching.

In my reading and learning, a bigger picture came into view about third parties and American politics. The story was not one of a series of individual vignettes about long-forgotten movements and political activists. The history of third parties is a single tale of the rise and fall of the myriad but constant currents in the American body politic, and the way it manifests itself again and again.

While it was difficult to select from amongst the countless movements calling themselves political parties throughout American history[53] certain criteria had to be laid down. It was decided that clear evidence of an impact on America's society, politics or economics had to exist. The benefit of this decision was that, for example, while a multitude of parties described themselves as Socialist in one way or another in their name, only the Socialist Party featured in this book can be said to have had any real impact on American politics and policies. Focusing on their impact upon the system, as broadly defined, also allowed me to include the first third party, the Anti-Masons, who might otherwise have been seen as a historically insignificant political party. However, due to their political innovations I was able to justifiably include a party that not only came first and rightly deserves to be included, but also brings such a fascinating historical narrative with it. Additionally,

---

[53] After all, the Tea Party is decidedly not a political party in its own right and yet employs the term.

after much debate, I also had to exclude some parties that would have resulted in excellent reading, such as the Dixiecrats, but which had little to no impact on national elections.[54]

The result is the list of parties included in this book. They represent the parties that responded to and influenced the changes throughout U.S. history that mark the major turning points in the development and evolution of the United States. Whether it was the Civil War and abolition, or labor reform and the New Deal, the fingerprints of these third parties can be seen. Ultimately, though, the decisions could be considered arbitrary. Academics and enthusiasts alike would be justified in claiming that one or more party did not belong while others were conspicuously missing from the book.

As I stated at the beginning, other books on third parties, either collectively or individually, do exist. I simply believed that they were either limited in scope or inadequate to fully explore the political and legal analysis of third parties in the United States within their respective exciting historical narratives. After all, each party featured here required the perusal of countless books and articles to distill each chapter. The works that I used for reference are excellent and a great way to follow-up on any one party that is of particular interest to the reader.

In sum, this book is a labor of love that taught the author precisely what he was hoping to learn that day many years ago when he wandered into a book store in New York City looking for a single book on the history of third parties. As a labor of love, and not some thesis or financially-backed project with a major

---

[54] Some could argue that the Dixiecrats presaged the shift of the South as a Democratic stronghold to a Republican one. That process was already underway and was the result of so many individual actions on the part of the federal government and both major parties that the Dixiecrats could not meet the standards established for the book.

publisher, the author had complete control over the product. The result is the product I desired and have enjoyed. I hope you have too.

Appendix A: Electoral Vote Results Maps

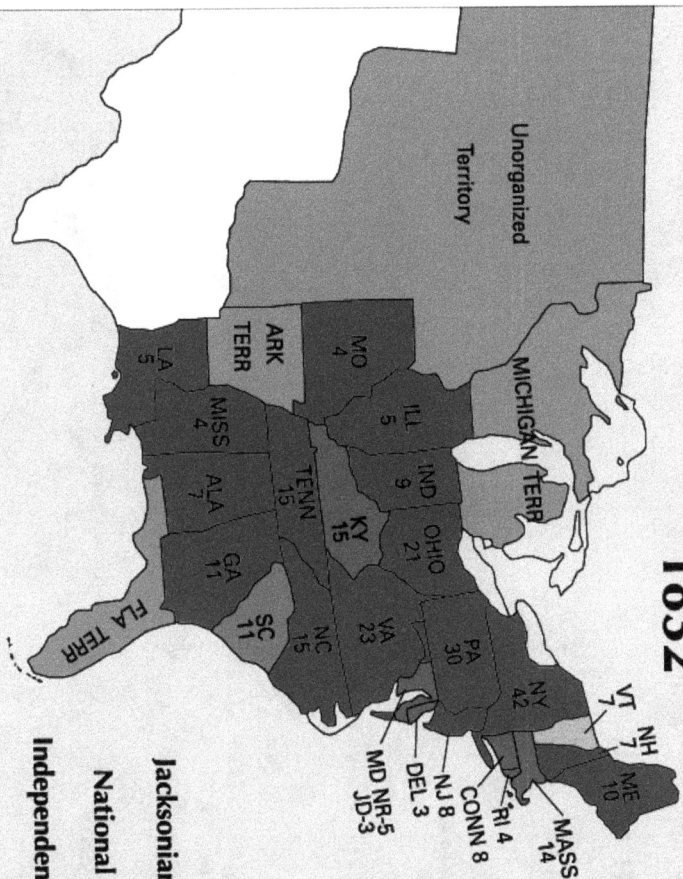

1832

Territories

Unorganized Territory

MICHIGAN TERR

ARK TERR

MO 4

ILL 5

IND 9

OHIO 21

KY 15

TENN 15

MISS 4

ALA 7

GA 11

SC 11

NC 15

VA 23

PA 30

NY 42

VT 7

NH 7

ME 10

MASS 14

RI 4

CONN 8

NJ 8

DEL 3

MD NR-5 JD-3

LA 5

FLA TERR

Jacksonian Democrat (Jackson)

National Republican (Clay)

Independent Democrat (Floyd)

Anti-Masonic (Wirt)

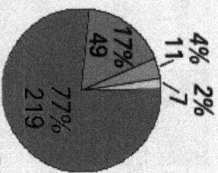

ELECTORAL VOTE
TOTAL VOTING: 286
NOT VOTING: 2

4% 2%
11 7
17%
49
77%
219

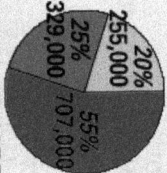

POPULAR VOTE
TOTAL: 1,291,000

20%
255,000

25%
329,000

55%
707,000

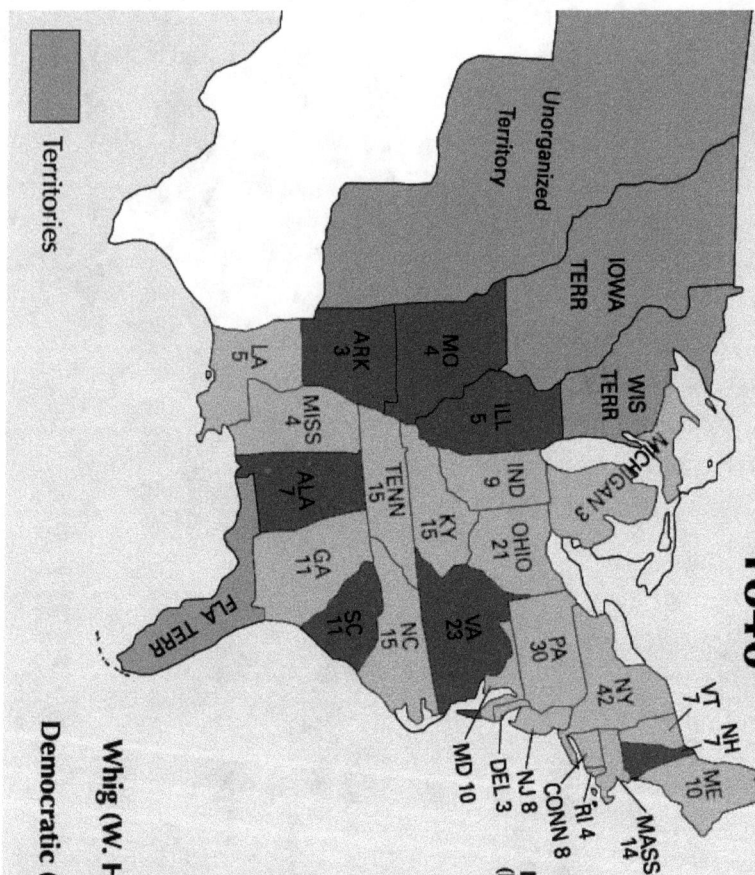

1840

Unorganized Territory

IOWA TERR

WIS TERR

MICHIGAN 3

LA 5

ARK 3

MO 4

ILL 5

IND 9

OHIO 21

MISS 4

ALA 7

TENN 15

KY 15

GA 11

FLA TERR

SC 11

NC 15

VA 23

PA 30

NY 42

VT 7

NH 7

ME 10

MASS 14

RI 4

CONN 8

NJ 8

DEL 3

MD 10

Territories

Whig (W. H. Harrison)

Democratic (Van Buren)

ELECTORAL VOTE
TOTAL: 294

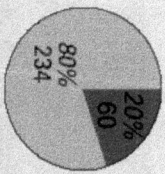

80% 234

20% 60

POPULAR VOTE
TOTAL: 2,411,187

LIBERTY (BIRNEY)
.25%
7,069

53%
1,275,016

46.75%
1,129,102

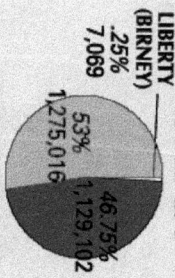

1844

Territories

Democratic (Polk)

Whig (Clay)

Unorganized Territory

IOWA TERR

WIS TERR

MICHIGAN 5

LA 6

ARK 3

MO 7

ILL 9

IND 12

OHIO 23

KY 12

TENN 13

MISS 6

ALA 9

GA 10

SC 9

NC 11

VA 17

PA 26

NY 36

VT 6

NH 6

ME 9

MASS 12

RI 4

CONN 6

NJ 7

DEL 3

MD 8

FLA TERR

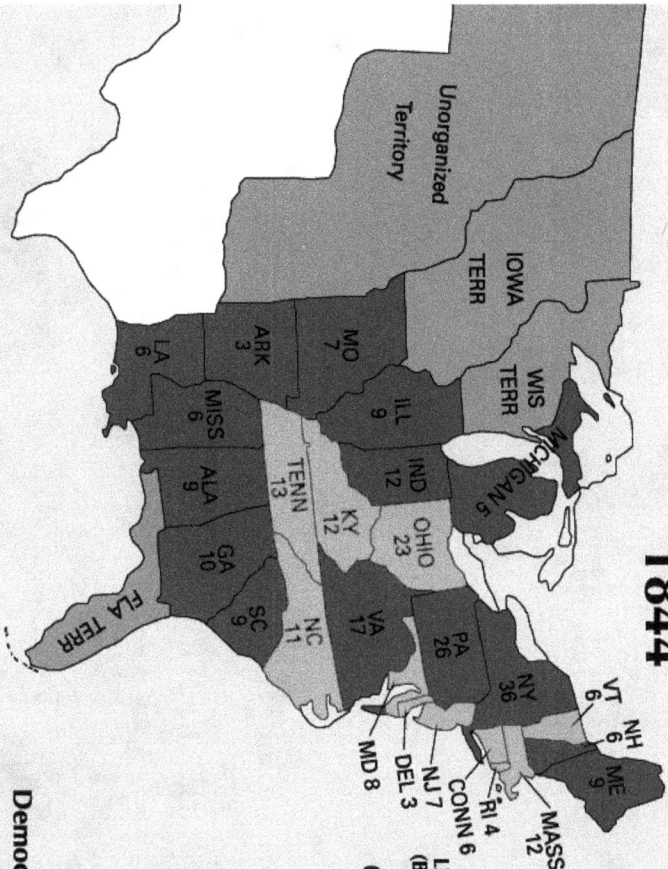

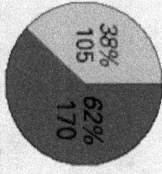

ELECTORAL VOTE
TOTAL: 275

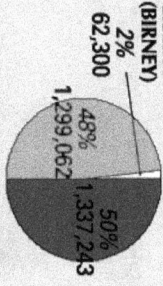

38% 105

62% 170

POPULAR VOTE
TOTAL: 2,698,605

LIBERTY (BIRNEY)
2% 62,300

48% 1,299,062

50% 1,337,243

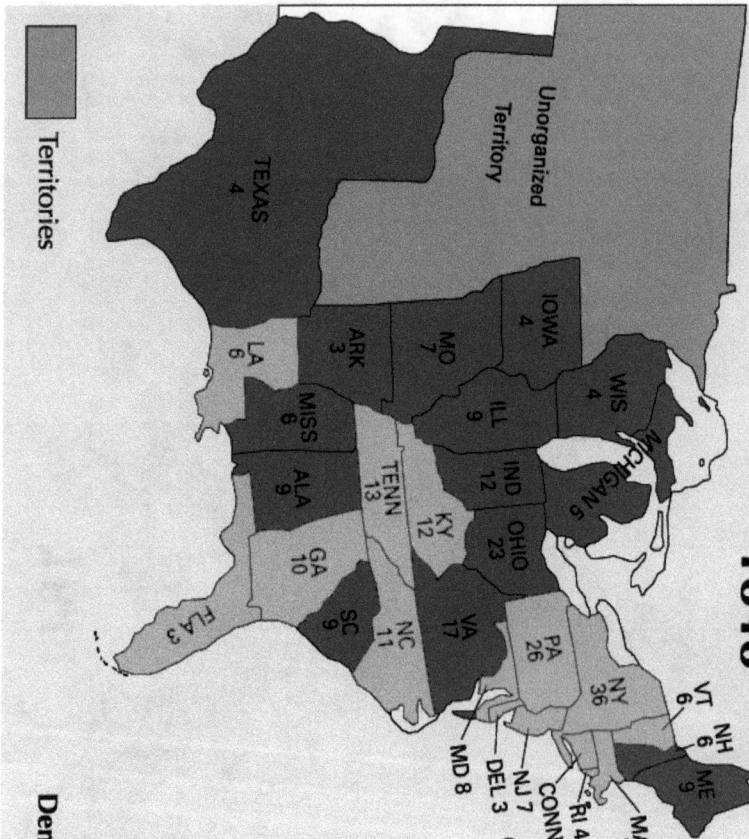

1848

Unorganized Territory

TEXAS 4

IOWA 4

LA 6 · ARK 3 · MO 7 · MISS 6 · ALA 9 · ILL 9 · WIS 4 · IND 12 · TENN 13 · KY 12 · OHIO 23 · MICHIGAN 5 · GA 10 · FLA 3 · SC 9 · NC 11 · VA 17 · PA 26 · NY 36 · VT 6 · NH 6 · ME 9 · MASS 12 · RI 4 · CONN 6 · NJ 7 · DEL 3 · MD 8

Territories

Whig (Taylor)

Democratic (Cass)

ELECTORAL VOTE
TOTAL: 290

56% 163
44% 127

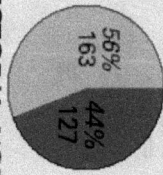

POPULAR VOTE
TOTAL: 2,871,906

FREE SOIL
(VAN BUREN)
10%
291,263

47.5%
1,360,099

42.5%
1,220,544

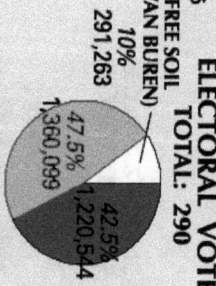

1892

Territories

CALIF D-8
OREGON R-3
WASH 4
NEVADA 3
IDAHO 3
MONTANA 3
WYOMING 3
UTAH TERR
ARIZONA TERR
NEW MEXICO TERR
COLORADO 4
CHEROKEE OUTLET
OKLA TERR
TEXAS 15
IND TERR
KANSAS 10
NEBRASKA 8
S DAK 4
N DAK D-1 R-1 P-1
MINN 9
IOWA 13
MO 17
ARK 8
LA 8
MISS 9
ALA 11
TENN 12
ILL 24
IND R-22 D-1
KY 13
GA 13
FLA 4
SC 9
NC 11
VA 12
W VA 6
OHIO R-22 D-1
PA 32
WIS 12
MICHIGAN D-5
NY 36
VT 4
NH 4
ME 6
MASS 15
RI 4
CONN 6
NJ 10
DEL 3
MD 8

ELECTORAL VOTE
TOTAL: 444

5%
22

33%
145

62%
277

POPULAR VOTE
TOTAL: 12,059,351

9%
1,041,028
MINOR 2%
285,297

43%
5,176,108

46%
5,556,918

Democratic (Cleveland)

Republican (B. Harrison)

Populist (Weaver)

191

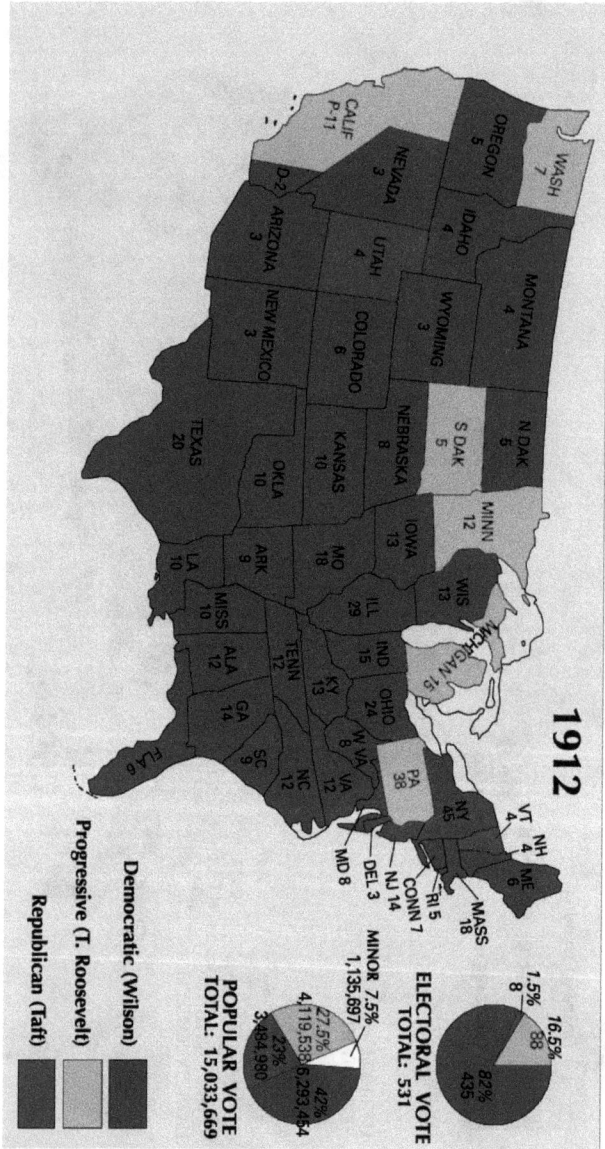

1912

State	Electoral Votes
WASH	7
OREGON	5
CALIF P-11	
NEVADA	3
IDAHO	4
UTAH	4
ARIZONA	3 D-2
NEW MEXICO	3
COLORADO	6
WYOMING	3
MONTANA	4
N. DAK	5
S DAK	5
NEBRASKA	8
KANSAS	10
OKLA	10
TEXAS	20
MINN	12
IOWA	13
MO	18
ARK	9
LA	10
MISS	10
ALA	12
WIS	13
ILL	29
IND	15
MICHIGAN	15
TENN	12
KY	13
OHIO	24
GA	14
FLA 6	
SC	9
NC	12
W VA	8
VA	12
PA	38
MD 8	
DEL 3	
NJ 14	
CONN 7	
RI 5	
NY	45
VT 4	
NH 4	
ME 4	
MASS 18	

Democratic (Wilson)

Progressive (T. Roosevelt)

Republican (Taft)

ELECTORAL VOTE
TOTAL: 531

16.5%
88

1.5%
8

82%
435

POPULAR VOTE
TOTAL: 15,033,669

MINOR 7.5%
1,135,697

27.5%
4,119,538

23%
3,484,980

42%
6,293,454

1924

CALIF 13
OREGON 5
WASH 7
NEVADA 3
IDAHO 4
MONTANA 4
ARIZONA 3
UTAH 4
WYOMING 3
NEW MEXICO 3
COLORADO 6
N DAK 5
S DAK 5
NEBRASKA 8
TEXAS 20
KANSAS 10
OKLA 10
MINN 12
IOWA 13
MO 18
WIS 13
MICHIGAN 15
LA 10
ARK 9
ILL 29
IND 15
OHIO 24
MISS 10
TENN 12
KY 13
ALA 12
GA 14
W VA 8
PA 38
FLA 6
SC 9
NC 12
VA 12
NY 45
VT 4
NH 4
ME 6
MASS 18
RI 5
CONN 7
NJ 14
DEL 3
MD 8

ELECTORAL VOTE
TOTAL: 531

2.5% 13
72% 382
25.5% 136

POPULAR VOTE
TOTAL: 29,090,208

16.5% 4,822,856
MINOR .5% 155,833
54% 15,725,016
29% 8,386,503

Republican (Coolidge)
Democratic (Davis)
Progressive (La Follette)

193

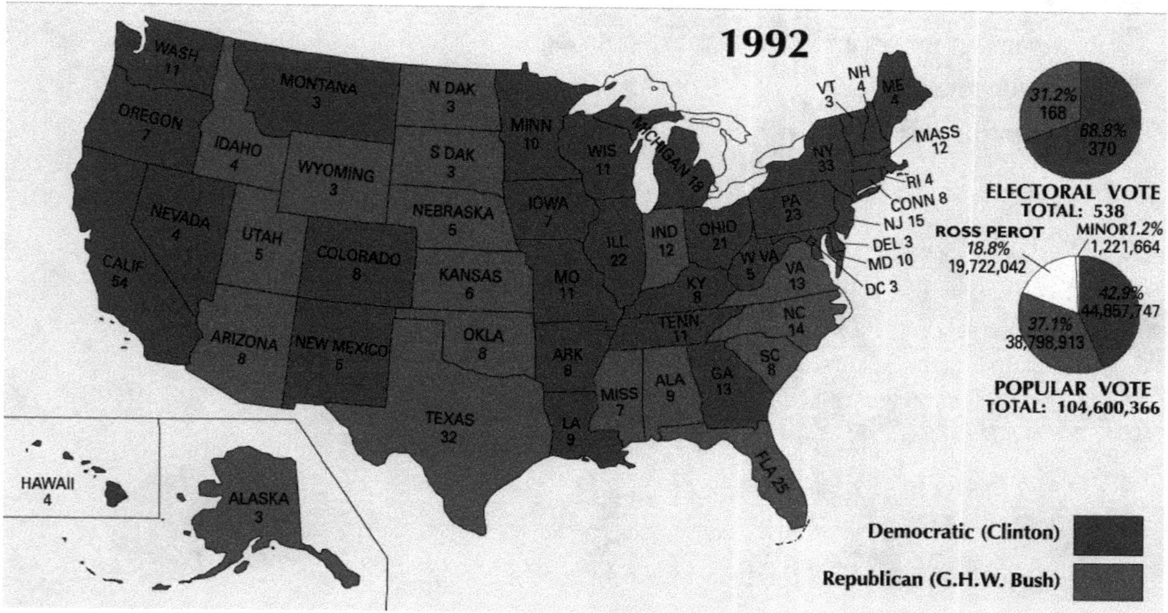
1992
WASH 11
OREGON 7
CALIF 54
NEVADA 4
IDAHO 4
MONTANA 3
WYOMING 3
UTAH 5
ARIZONA 8
COLORADO 8
NEW MEXICO 5
N DAK 3
S DAK 3
NEBRASKA 5
KANSAS 6
OKLA 8
TEXAS 32
MINN 10
IOWA 7
MO 11
ARK 6
LA 9
WIS 11
ILL 22
MICHIGAN 18
IND 12
OHIO 21
KY 8
TENN 11
MISS 7
ALA 9
GA 13
FLA 25
SC 8
NC 14
VA 13
W VA 5
PA 23
NY 33
VT 3
NH 4
ME 4
MASS 12
RI 4
CONN 8
NJ 15
DEL 3
MD 10
DC 3
HAWAII 4
ALASKA 3
31.2% 168
68.8% 370
ELECTORAL VOTE
TOTAL: 538
ROSS PEROT 18.8% 19,722,042
MINOR 1.2% 1,221,664
42.9% 44,857,747
37.1% 38,798,913
POPULAR VOTE
TOTAL: 104,600,366
Democratic (Clinton)
Republican (G.H.W. Bush)

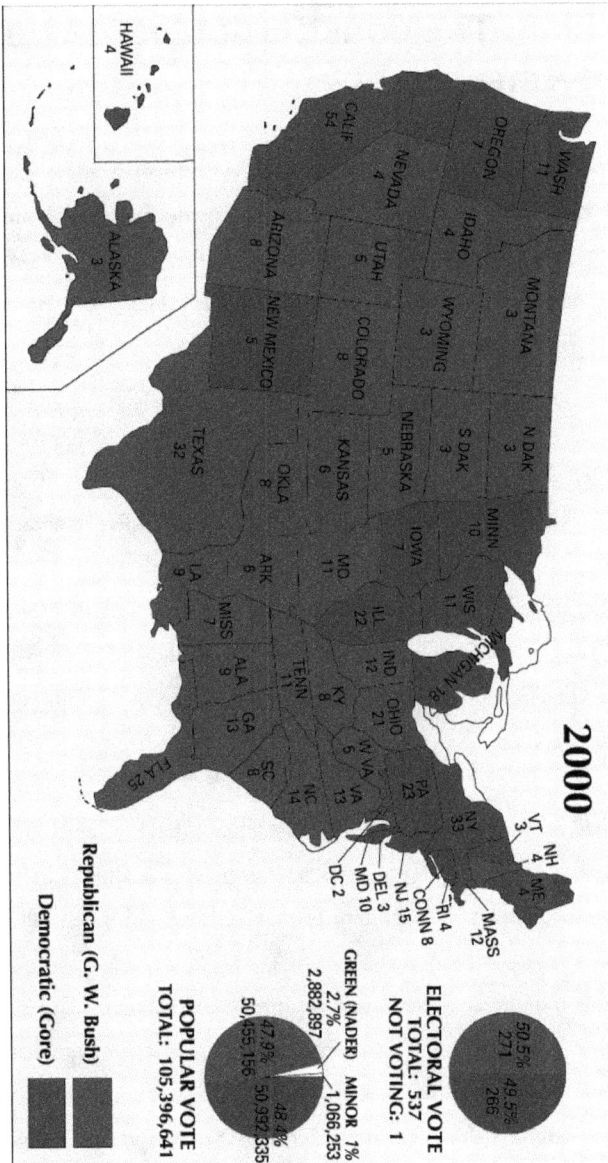

2000

HAWAII 4
ALASKA 3

WASH 11
OREGON 7
CALIF 54
NEVADA 4
IDAHO 4
MONTANA 3
ARIZONA 5
UTAH 5
WYOMING 3
N. DAK 3
S. DAK 3
NEW MEXICO 5
COLORADO 8
NEBRASKA 5
KANSAS 6
MINN 10
IOWA 7
WIS 11
MICHIGAN 18
TEXAS 32
OKLA 8
MO 11
ILL 22
IND 12
OHIO 21
LA 9
ARK 6
MISS 7
ALA 9
TENN 11
KY 8
W.VA 5
VA 13
NC 14
SC 8
GA 13
FLA 25
PA 23
NY 33
VT 3
NH 4
ME 4
MASS 12
RI 4
CONN 8
NJ 15
DEL 3
MD 10
DC 2

Republican (G. W. Bush)

Democratic (Gore)

ELECTORAL VOTE
TOTAL: 537
NOT VOTING: 1

50.5% 271
49.5% 266

POPULAR VOTE
TOTAL: 105,396,641

GREEN (NADER) 2.7%
2,882,897

MINOR 1%
1,066,253

47.9%
50,455,156

48.4%
50,992,335

195

Appendix B: The Constitution of the United States of America

We the People of the United States, in Order to form a more perfect Union, establish Justice, insure domestic Tranquility, provide for the common defence, promote the general Welfare, and secure the Blessings of Liberty to ourselves and our Posterity, do ordain and establish this Constitution for the United States of America.

Article 1

Section 1. All legislative Powers herein granted shall be vested in a Congress of the United States, which shall consist of a Senate and House of Representatives.

Section 2. The House of Representatives shall be composed of Members chosen every second Year by the People of the several States, and the Electors in each State shall have the Qualifications requisite for Electors of the most numerous Branch of the State Legislature.

No Person shall be a Representative who shall not have attained to the age of twenty five Years, and been seven Years a Citizen of the United States, and who shall not, when elected, be an Inhabitant of that State in which he shall be chosen.

Representatives and direct Taxes shall be apportioned among the several States which may be included within this Union, according to their respective Numbers, which shall be determined by adding to the whole Number of free Persons, including those bound to Service for a Term of Years, and excluding Indians not taxed, three fifths of all other Persons. The actual Enumeration shall be made within three Years after the first Meeting of the Congress of the United States, and within every subsequent Term of ten Years, in such Manner as they shall by Law direct. The Number of Representatives shall not exceed one for every thirty Thousand, but each State shall have at Least one Representative; and until such enumeration shall be made, the State of New Hampshire shall be entitled to chuse three, Massachusetts eight, Rhode-Island and Providence Plantations one, Connecticut five, New-York six, New Jersey four, Pennsylvania eight, Delaware one, Maryland six, Virginia ten, North Carolina five, South Carolina five, and Georgia three.

When vacancies happen in the Representation from any State, the Executive Authority thereof shall issue Writs of Election to fill such Vacancies.

The House of Representatives shall chuse their Speaker and other Officers; and shall have the sole Power of Impeachment.

Section 3. The Senate of the United States shall be composed of two Senators from each State, chosen by the Legislature thereof, for six Years; and each Senator shall have one Vote.

Immediately after they shall be assembled in Consequence of the first Election, they shall be divided as equally as may be into three Classes. The Seats of the Senators of the first Class shall be vacated at the Expiration of the second Year, of the second Class at the Expiration of the fourth Year, and the third Class at the Expiration of the sixth Year, so that one third may be chosen every second Year; and if Vacancies happen by Resignation, or otherwise, during the Recess of the Legislature of any State, the Executive thereof may make temporary Appointments until the next Meeting of the Legislature, which shall then fill such Vacancies.

No Person shall be a Senator who shall not have attained to the Age of thirty Years, and been nine Years a Citizen of the United States and who shall not, when elected, be an Inhabitant of that State for which he shall be chosen.

The Vice President of the United States shall be President of the Senate, but shall have no Vote, unless they be equally divided.

The Senate shall chuse their other Officers, and also a President pro tempore, in the Absence of the Vice President, or when he shall exercise the Office of President of the United States.

The Senate shall have the sole Power to try all Impeachments. When sitting for that Purpose, they shall be on Oath or Affirmation. When the President of the United States is tried, the Chief Justice shall preside: And no Person shall be convicted without the Concurrence of two thirds of the Members present.

Judgment in Cases of Impeachment shall not extend further than to removal from Office, and disqualification to hold and enjoy any Office of Honor, Trust or Profit under the United States: but the Party convicted shall nevertheless be liable and subject to Indictment, Trial, Judgment and Punishment, according to Law.

Section 4. The Times, Places and Manner of holding Elections for Senators and Representatives, shall be prescribed in each State by the Legislature thereof; but the Congress may at any time by Law make or alter such Regulations, except as to the Places of chusing Senators.

The Congress shall assemble at least once in every Year, and such Meeting shall be on the first Monday in December, unless they shall by Law appoint a different Day.

Section 5. Each House shall be the Judge of the Elections, Returns and Qualifications of its own Members, and a Majority of each shall constitute a Quorum to do Business; but a smaller Number may adjourn from day to day, and may be authorized to compel the Attendance of absent Members, in such Manner, and under such Penalties as each House may provide.

Each House may determine the Rules of its Proceedings, punish its Members for disorderly Behaviour, and, with the Concurrence of two thirds, expel a Member.

Each House shall keep a Journal of its Proceedings, and from time to time publish the same, excepting such Parts as may in their Judgment require Secrecy; and the Yeas and Nays of the Members of either House on any question shall, at the Desire of one fifth of those Present, be entered on the Journal.

Neither House, during the Session of Congress, shall, without the Consent of the other, adjourn for more than three days, nor to any other Place than that in which the two Houses shall be sitting.

Section 6. The Senators and Representatives shall receive a Compensation for their Services, to be ascertained by Law, and paid out of the Treasury of the United States. They shall in all Cases, except Treason, Felony and Breach of the Peace, be privileged from Arrest during their Attendance at the Session of their respective Houses, and in going to and returning from the same; and for any Speech or Debate in either House, they shall not be questioned in any other Place.

No Senator or Representative shall, during the Time for which he was elected, be appointed to any civil Office under the Authority of the United States, which shall have been created, or the Emoluments whereof shall have been encreased during such time: and no Person holding any Office under the United States, shall be a Member of either House during his Continuance in Office.

Section 7. All Bills for raising Revenue shall originate in the House of Representatives; but the Senate may propose or concur with Amendments as on other Bills.

Every Bill which shall have passed the House of Representatives and the Senate, shall, before it become a Law, be presented to the President of the United States; if he approve he shall sign it, but if not he shall return it, with his Objections to that House in which it shall have originated, who shall enter the Objections at large on their Journal, and proceed to reconsider it. If after such Reconsideration two thirds of that House shall agree to pass the Bill, it shall be sent, together with the Objections, to the other House, by which it shall likewise be reconsidered, and if approved by two thirds of that House, it shall become a Law. But in all such Cases the Votes of both Houses shall be determined by Yeas and Nays, and the Names of the Persons voting for and against the Bill shall be entered on the Journal of each House respectively. If any Bill shall not be returned by the President within ten Days (Sundays excepted) after it shall have been presented to him, the Same shall be a Law, in like Manner as if he had signed it, unless the Congress by their Adjournment prevent its Return, in which Case it shall not be a Law.

Every Order, Resolution, or Vote to which the Concurrence of the Senate and House of Representatives may be necessary (except on a question of Adjournment) shall be presented to the President of the United States; and before the Same shall take Effect, shall be approved by him, or being disapproved by him, shall be repassed by two thirds of the Senate and House of Representatives, according to the Rules and Limitations prescribed in the Case of a Bill.

Section 8. The Congress shall have Power To lay and collect Taxes, Duties, Imposts and Excises, to pay the Debts and provide for the common Defence and general Welfare of the United States; but all Duties, Imposts and Excises shall be uniform throughout the United States;

To borrow Money on the credit of the United States;

To regulate Commerce with foreign Nations, and among the several States, and with the Indian Tribes;

To establish an uniform Rule of Naturalization, and uniform Laws on the subject of Bankruptcies throughout the United States;

To coin Money, regulate the Value thereof, and of foreign Coin, and fix the Standard of Weights and Measures;

To provide for the Punishment of counterfeiting the Securities and current Coin of the United States;

To establish Post Offices and post Roads;

To promote the Progress of Science and useful Arts, by securing for limited Times to Authors and Inventors the exclusive Right to their respective Writings and Discoveries;

To constitute Tribunals inferior to the supreme Court;

To define and punish Piracies and Felonies committed on the high Seas, and Offences against the Law of Nations;

To declare War, grant Letters of Marque and Reprisal, and make Rules concerning Captures on Land and Water;

To raise and support Armies, but no Appropriation of Money to that Use shall be for a longer Term than two Years;

To provide and maintain a Navy;

To make Rules for the Government and Regulation of the land and naval Forces;

To provide for calling forth the Militia to execute the Laws of the Union, suppress Insurrections and repel Invasions;

To provide for organizing, arming, and disciplining, the Militia, and for governing such Part of them as may be employed in the Service of the United States, reserving to the States respectively, the Appointment of the Officers, and the Authority of training the Militia according to the discipline prescribed by Congress;

To exercise exclusive Legislation in all Cases whatsoever, over such District (not exceeding ten Miles square) as may, by Cession of particular States, and the Acceptance of Congress, become the Seat of the Government of the United States, and to exercise like Authority over all Places purchased by the Consent of the Legislature of the State in which the Same shall be, for the Erection of Forts, Magazines, Arsenals, dock-Yards, and other needful Buildings;--And

To make all Laws which shall be necessary and proper for carrying into Execution the foregoing Powers, and all other Powers vested by this Constitution in the Government of the United States, or in any Department or Officer thereof.

Section 9. The Migration or Importation of such Persons as any of the States now existing shall think proper to admit, shall not be prohibited by the Congress prior to the Year one thousand eight hundred and eight, but a Tax or duty may be imposed on such Importation, not exceeding ten dollars for each Person.

The Privilege of the Writ of Habeas Corpus shall not be suspended, unless when in Cases of Rebellion or Invasion the public Safety may require it.

No Bill of Attainder or ex post facto Law shall be passed.

No Capitation, or other direct, Tax shall be laid, unless in Proportion to the Census or Enumeration herein before directed to be taken.

No Tax or Duty shall be laid on Articles exported from any State.

No Preference shall be given by any Regulation of Commerce or Revenue to the Ports of one State over those of another: nor shall Vessels bound to, or from, one State, be obliged to enter, clear or pay Duties in another.

No Money shall be drawn from the Treasury, but in Consequence of Appropriations made by Law; and a regular Statement and Account of Receipts and Expenditures of all public Money shall be published from time to time.

No Title of Nobility shall be granted by the United States: And no Person holding any Office of Profit or Trust under them, shall, without the Consent of the Congress, accept of any present, Emolument, Office, or Title, of any kind whatever, from any King, Prince, or foreign State.

Section 10. No State shall enter into any Treaty, Alliance, or Confederation; grant Letters of Marque and Reprisal; coin Money; emit Bills of Credit; make any Thing but gold and silver Coin a Tender in Payment of Debts; pass any Bill of Attainder, ex post facto Law, or Law impairing the Obligation of Contracts, or grant any Title of Nobility.

No State shall, without the Consent of the Congress, lay any Imposts or Duties on Imports or Exports, except what may be absolutely necessary for executing it's inspection Laws: and the net Produce of all Duties and Imposts, laid by any State on Imports or Exports, shall be for the Use of the Treasury of the United States; and all such Laws shall be subject to the Revision and Controul of the Congress.

No State shall, without the Consent of Congress, lay any Duty of Tonnage, keep Troops, or Ships of War in time of Peace, enter into any Agreement or Compact with another State, or with a foreign Power, or engage in War, unless actually invaded, or in such imminent Danger as will not admit of delay.

Article II

Section 1. The executive Power shall be vested in a President of the United States of America. He shall hold his Office during the Term of four Years, and, together with the Vice President, chosen for the same Term, be elected, as follows:

Each State shall appoint, in such Manner as the Legislature thereof may direct, a Number of Electors, equal to the whole Number of Senators and Representatives to which the State may be entitled in the Congress: but no Senator or Representative, or Person holding an Office of Trust or Profit under the United States, shall be appointed an Elector.

The Electors shall meet in their respective States, and vote by Ballot for two Persons, of whom one at least shall not be an Inhabitant of the same State with themselves. And they shall make a List of all the Persons voted for, and of the Number of Votes for each; which List they shall sign and certify, and transmit sealed to the Seat of the Government of the United States, directed to the President of the Senate. The President of the Senate shall, in the Presence of the Senate and House of Representatives, open all the Certificates, and the Votes shall then be counted. The Person having the greatest Number of Votes shall be the President, if such Number be a Majority of the whole Number of Electors appointed; and if there be more than one who have such Majority, and have an equal Number of Votes, then the House of Representatives shall immediately chuse by Ballot one of them for President; and if no Person have a Majority, then from the five highest on the List the said House shall in like Manner chuse the President. But in chusing the

President, the Votes shall be taken by States, the Representation from each State having one Vote; A quorum for this Purpose shall consist of a Member or Members from two thirds of the States, and a Majority of all the States shall be necessary to a Choice. In every Case, after the Choice of the President, the Person having the greatest Number of Votes of the Electors shall be the Vice President. But if there should remain two or more who have equal Votes, the Senate shall chuse from them by Ballot the Vice President.

The Congress may determine the Time of chusing the Electors, and the Day on which they shall give their Votes; which Day shall be the same throughout the United States.

No Person except a natural born Citizen, or a Citizen of the United States, at the time of the Adoption of this Constitution, shall be eligible to the Office of President; neither shall any Person be eligible to that Office who shall not have attained to the Age of thirty five Years, and been fourteen Years a Resident within the United States.

In Case of the Removal of the President from Office, or of his Death, Resignation, or Inability to discharge the Powers and Duties of the said Office, the Same shall devolve on the Vice President, and the Congress may by Law provide for the Case of Removal, Death, Resignation or Inability, both of the President and Vice President, declaring what Officer shall then act as President, and such Officer shall act accordingly, until the Disability be removed, or a President shall be elected.

The President shall, at stated Times, receive for his Services, a Compensation, which shall neither be encreased nor diminished during the Period for which he shall have been elected, and he shall not receive within that Period any other Emolument from the United States, or any of them.

Before he enter on the Execution of his Office, he shall take the following Oath or Affirmation:--"I do solemnly swear (or affirm) that I will faithfully execute the Office of President of the United States, and will to the best of my Ability, preserve, protect and defend the Constitution of the United States."

Section 2. The President shall be Commander in Chief of the Army and Navy of the United States, and of the Militia of the several States, when called into the actual Service of the United States; he may require the Opinion, in writing, of the principal Officer in each of the executive Departments, upon any Subject relating to the Duties of their respective Offices, and he shall have Power to grant Reprieves and Pardons for Offences against the United States, except in Cases of Impeachment.

He shall have Power, by and with the Advice and Consent of the Senate, to make Treaties, provided two thirds of the Senators present concur; and he shall nominate, and by and with the Advice and Consent of the Senate, shall appoint Ambassadors, other public Ministers and Consuls, Judges of the supreme Court, and all other Officers of the United States, whose Appointments are not herein otherwise provided for, and which shall be established by Law: but the Congress may by Law vest the Appointment of such inferior Officers, as they think proper, in the President alone, in the Courts of Law, or in the Heads of Departments.

The President shall have Power to fill up all Vacancies that may happen during the Recess of the Senate, by granting Commissions which shall expire at the End of their next Session.

Section 3. He shall from time to time give to the Congress Information of the State of the Union, and recommend to their Consideration such Measures as he shall judge necessary and expedient; he may, on extraordinary Occasions, convene both Houses, or either of them, and in Case of Disagreement between them, with Respect to the Time of Adjournment, he may adjourn them to such Time as he shall think proper; he shall receive Ambassadors and other public Ministers; he shall take Care that the Laws be faithfully executed, and shall Commission all the Officers of the United States.

Section 4. The President, Vice President and all civil Officers of the United States, shall be removed from Office on Impeachment for, and Conviction of, Treason, Bribery, or other high Crimes and Misdemeanors.
Article III

Section 1. The judicial Power of the United States, shall be vested in one supreme Court, and in such inferior Courts as the Congress may from time to time ordain and establish. The Judges, both of the supreme and inferior Courts, shall hold their Offices during good Behaviour, and shall, at stated Times, receive for their Services, a Compensation, which shall not be diminished during their Continuance in Office.

Section 2. The judicial Power shall extend to all Cases, in Law and Equity, arising under this Constitution, the Laws of the United States, and Treaties made, or which shall be made, under their Authority;--to all Cases affecting Ambassadors, other public Ministers and Consuls;--to all Cases of admiralty and maritime Jurisdiction;-- to Controversies to which the United States shall be a Party;--to Controversies between two or more States;--between a State and Citizens of another State;-- between Citizens of different States;--between Citizens of the same State claiming Lands under Grants of different States, and between a State, or the Citizens thereof, and foreign States, Citizens or Subjects.

In all Cases affecting Ambassadors, other public Ministers and Consuls, and those in which a State shall be Party, the supreme Court shall have original Jurisdiction. In all the other Cases before mentioned, the supreme Court shall have appellate Jurisdiction, both as to Law and Fact, with such Exceptions, and under such Regulations as the Congress shall make.

The Trial of all Crimes, except in Cases of Impeachment, shall be by Jury; and such Trial shall be held in the State where the said Crimes shall have been committed; but when not committed within any State, the Trial shall be at such Place or Places as the Congress may by Law have directed.

Section 3. Treason against the United States, shall consist only in levying War against them, or in adhering to their Enemies, giving them Aid and Comfort. No Person shall be convicted of Treason unless on the Testimony of two Witnesses to the same overt Act, or on Confession in open Court.

The Congress shall have Power to declare the Punishment of Treason, but no Attainder of Treason shall work Corruption of Blood, or Forfeiture except during the Life of the Person attainted.

Article IV

Section 1. Full Faith and Credit shall be given in each State to the public Acts, Records, and judicial Proceedings of every other State. And the Congress may by general Laws prescribe the Manner in which such Acts, Records, and Proceedings shall be proved, and the Effect thereof.

Section 2. The Citizens of each State shall be entitled to all Privileges and Immunities of Citizens in the several States.

A Person charged in any State with Treason, Felony, or other Crime, who shall flee from Justice, and be found in another State, shall on Demand of the executive Authority of the State from which he fled, be delivered up, to be removed to the State having Jurisdiction of the Crime.

No Person held to Service or Labour in one State, under the Laws thereof, escaping into another, shall, in Consequence of any Law or Regulation therein, be discharged from such Service or Labour, but shall be delivered up on Claim of the Party to whom such Service or Labour may be due.

Section 3. New States may be admitted by the Congress into this Union; but no new States shall be formed or erected within the Jurisdiction of any other State; nor any State be formed by the Junction of two or more States, or Parts of States, without the Consent of the Legislatures of the States concerned as well as of the Congress.

The Congress shall have Power to dispose of and make all needful Rules and Regulations respecting the Territory or other Property belonging to the United

States; and nothing in this Constitution shall be so construed as to Prejudice any Claims of the United States, or of any particular State.

Section 4. The United States shall guarantee to every State in this Union a Republican Form of Government, and shall protect each of them against Invasion; and on Application of the Legislature, or of the Executive (when the Legislature cannot be convened) against domestic Violence.

Article V

The Congress, whenever two thirds of both Houses shall deem it necessary, shall propose Amendments to this Constitution, or, on the Application of the Legislatures of two thirds of the several States, shall call a Convention for proposing Amendments, which, in either Case, shall be valid to all Intents and Purposes, as Part of this Constitution, when ratified by the Legislatures of three fourths of the several States, or by Conventions in three fourths thereof, as the one or the other Mode of Ratification may be proposed by the Congress; Provided that no Amendment which may be made prior to the Year One thousand eight hundred and eight shall in any Manner affect the first and fourth Clauses in the Ninth Section of the first Article; and that no State, without its Consent, shall be deprived of its equal Suffrage in the Senate.

Article VI

All Debts contracted and Engagements entered into, before the Adoption of this Constitution, shall be as valid against the United States under this Constitution, as under the Confederation.

This Constitution, and the Laws of the United States which shall be made in Pursuance thereof; and all Treaties made, or which shall be made, under the Authority of the United States, shall be the supreme Law of the Land; and the Judges in every State shall be bound thereby, any Thing in the Constitution or Laws of any State to the Contrary notwith-standing.

The Senators and Representatives before mentioned, and the Members of the several State Legislatures, and all executive and judicial Officers, both of the United States and of the several States, shall be bound by Oath or Affirmation, to support this Constitution; but no religious Test shall ever be required as a Qualification to any Office or public Trust under the United States.
Article VII

The Ratification of the Conventions of nine States, shall be sufficient for the Establishment of this Constitution between the States so ratifying the Same.

Done in Convention by the Unanimous Consent of the States present the Seventeenth Day of September in the Year of our Lord one thousand seven hundred and Eighty seven and of the Independence of the United States of America the Twelfth

In witness whereof We have hereunto subscribed our Names,

George Washington--President and deputy from Virginia

New Hampshire: John Langdon, Nicholas Gilman

Massachusetts: Nathaniel Gorham, Rufus King

Connecticut: William Samuel Johnson, Roger Sherman

New York: Alexander Hamilton

New Jersey: William Livingston, David Brearly, William Paterson, Jonathan Dayton

Pennsylvania: Benjamin Franklin, Thomas Mifflin, Robert Morris, George Clymer, Thomas FitzSimons, Jared Ingersoll, James Wilson, Gouverneur Morris

Delaware: George Read, Gunning Bedford, Jr., John Dickinson, Richard Bassett, Jacob Broom

Maryland: James McHenry, Daniel of Saint Thomas Jenifer, Daniel Carroll

Virginia: John Blair, James Madison, Jr.

North Carolina: William Blount, Richard Dobbs Spaight, Hugh Williamson

South Carolina: John Rutledge, Charles Cotesworth Pinckney, Charles Pinckney, Pierce Butler

Georgia: William Few, Abraham Baldwin

THE BILL OF RIGHTS:
Amendment 1 - Freedom of Religion, Press, Expression.

Congress shall make no law respecting an establishment of religion, or prohibiting the free exercise thereof; or abridging the freedom of speech, or of the press; or the right of the people peaceably to assemble, and to petition the Government for a redress of grievances.

Amendment 2 - Right to Bear Arms.

A well regulated Militia, being necessary to the security of a free State, the right of the people to keep and bear Arms, shall not be infringed.

Amendment 3 - Quartering of Soldiers.

No Soldier shall, in time of peace be quartered in any house, without the consent of the Owner, nor in time of war, but in a manner to be prescribed by law.

Amendment 4 - Search and Seizure.

The right of the people to be secure in their persons, houses, papers, and effects, against unreasonable searches and seizures, shall not be violated, and no Warrants shall issue, but upon probable cause, supported by Oath or affirmation, and particularly describing the place to be searched, and the persons or things to be seized.

Amendment 5 - Trial and Punishment, Compensation for Takings.

No person shall be held to answer for a capital, or otherwise infamous crime, unless on a presentment or indictment of a Grand Jury, except in cases arising in the land or naval forces, or in the Militia, when in actual service in time of War or public danger; nor shall any person be subject for the same offense to be twice put in jeopardy of life or limb; nor shall be compelled in any criminal case to be a witness against himself, nor be deprived of life, liberty, or property, without due process of law; nor shall private property be taken for public use, without just compensation.

Amendment 6 - Right to Speedy Trial, Confrontation of Witnesses.

In all criminal prosecutions, the accused shall enjoy the right to a speedy and public trial, by an impartial jury of the State and district wherein the crime shall have been committed, which district shall have been previously ascertained by law, and to be informed of the nature and cause of the accusation; to be confronted with the witnesses against him; to have compulsory process for obtaining witnesses in his favor, and to have the Assistance of Counsel for his defence.

Amendment 7 - Trial by Jury in Civil Cases.

In Suits at common law, where the value in controversy shall exceed twenty dollars, the right of trial by jury shall be preserved, and no fact tried by a jury, shall be otherwise re-examined in any Court of the United States, than according to the rules of the common law.

Amendment 8 - Cruel and Unusual Punishment.

Excessive bail shall not be required, nor excessive fines imposed, nor cruel and unusual punishments inflicted.

Amendment 9 - Construction of Constitution.

The enumeration in the Constitution, of certain rights, shall not be construed to deny or disparage others retained by the people.

Amendment 10 - Powers of the States and People.

The powers not delegated to the United States by the Constitution, nor prohibited by it to the States, are reserved to the States respectively, or to the people.

ADDITIONAL AMENDMENTS TO THE U.S. CONSTITUTION:

Amendment 11 - Judicial Limits.

The Judicial power of the United States shall not be construed to extend to any suit in law or equity, commenced or prosecuted against one of the United States by Citizens of another State, or by Citizens or Subjects of any Foreign State.

Amendment 12 - Choosing the President, Vice-President.

The Electors shall meet in their respective states, and vote by ballot for President and Vice-President, one of whom, at least, shall not be an inhabitant of the same state with themselves; they shall name in their ballots the person voted for as President, and in distinct ballots the person voted for as Vice-President, and they

216

shall make distinct lists of all persons voted for as President, and of all persons voted for as Vice-President and of the number of votes for each, which lists they shall sign and certify, and transmit sealed to the seat of the government of the United States, directed to the President of the Senate;

The President of the Senate shall, in the presence of the Senate and House of Representatives, open all the certificates and the votes shall then be counted;

The person having the greatest Number of votes for President, shall be the President, if such number be a majority of the whole number of Electors appointed; and if no person have such majority, then from the persons having the highest numbers not exceeding three on the list of those voted for as President, the House of Representatives shall choose immediately, by ballot, the President. But in choosing the President, the votes shall be taken by states, the representation from each state having one vote; a quorum for this purpose shall consist of a member or members from two-thirds of the states, and a majority of all the states shall be necessary to a choice. And if the House of Representatives shall not choose a President whenever the right of choice shall devolve upon them, before the fourth day of March next following, then the Vice-President shall act as President, as in the case of the death or other constitutional disability of the President.

The person having the greatest number of votes as Vice-President, shall be the Vice-President, if such number be a majority of the whole number of Electors appointed, and if no person have a majority, then from the two highest numbers on the list, the Senate shall choose the Vice-President; a quorum for the purpose shall consist of two-thirds of the whole number of Senators, and a majority of the whole number shall be necessary to a choice. But no person constitutionally ineligible to the office of President shall be eligible to that of Vice-President of the United States.

Amendment 13 - Slavery Abolished.

1. Neither slavery nor involuntary servitude, except as a punishment for crime whereof the party shall have been duly convicted, shall exist within the United States, or any place subject to their jurisdiction.

2. Congress shall have power to enforce this article by appropriate legislation.

Amendment 14 - Citizenship Rights.

1. All persons born or naturalized in the United States, and subject to the jurisdiction thereof, are citizens of the United States and of the State wherein they reside. No State shall make or enforce any law which shall abridge the privileges or immunities of citizens of the United States; nor shall any State deprive any person of life, liberty, or property, without due process of law; nor deny to any person within its jurisdiction the equal protection of the laws.

2. Representatives shall be apportioned among the several States according to their respective numbers, counting the whole number of persons in each State, excluding Indians not taxed. But when the right to vote at any election for the choice of electors for President and Vice-President of the United States, Representatives in Congress, the Executive and Judicial officers of a State, or the members of the Legislature thereof, is denied to any of the male inhabitants of such State, being twenty-one years of age, and citizens of the United States, or in any way abridged,

except for participation in rebellion, or other crime, the basis of representation therein shall be reduced in the proportion which the number of such male citizens shall bear to the whole number of male citizens twenty-one years of age in such State.

3. No person shall be a Senator or Representative in Congress, or elector of President and Vice-President, or hold any office, civil or military, under the United States, or under any State, who, having previously taken an oath, as a member of Congress, or as an officer of the United States, or as a member of any State legislature, or as an executive or judicial officer of any State, to support the Constitution of the United States, shall have engaged in insurrection or rebellion against the same, or given aid or comfort to the enemies thereof. But Congress may by a vote of two-thirds of each House, remove such disability.

4. The validity of the public debt of the United States, authorized by law, including debts incurred for payment of pensions and bounties for services in suppressing insurrection or rebellion, shall not be questioned. But neither the United States nor any State shall assume or pay any debt or obligation incurred in aid of insurrection or rebellion against the United States, or any claim for the loss or emancipation of any slave; but all such debts, obligations and claims shall be held illegal and void.

5. The Congress shall have power to enforce, by appropriate legislation, the provisions of this article.

Amendment 15 - Race No Bar to Vote.

1. The right of citizens of the United States to vote shall not be denied or abridged by the United States or by any State on account of race, color, or previous condition of servitude.

2. The Congress shall have power to enforce this article by appropriate legislation. Amendment 16 - Status of Income Tax Clarified.

The Congress shall have power to lay and collect taxes on incomes, from whatever source derived, without apportionment among the several States, and without regard to any census or enumeration.

Amendment 17 - Senators Elected by Popular Vote.

The Senate of the United States shall be composed of two Senators from each State, elected by the people thereof, for six years; and each Senator shall have one vote. The electors in each State shall have the qualifications requisite for electors of the most numerous branch of the State legislatures.

When vacancies happen in the representation of any State in the Senate, the executive authority of such State shall issue writs of election to fill such vacancies: Provided, That the legislature of any State may empower the executive thereof to make temporary appointments until the people fill the vacancies by election as the legislature may direct.

This amendment shall not be so construed as to affect the election or term of any Senator chosen before it becomes valid as part of the Constitution.

Amendment 18 - Liquor Abolished.

1. After one year from the ratification of this article the manufacture, sale, or transportation of intoxicating liquors within, the importation thereof into, or the exportation thereof from the United States and all territory subject to the jurisdiction thereof for beverage purposes is hereby prohibited.

2. The Congress and the several States shall have concurrent power to enforce this article by appropriate legislation.

3. This article shall be inoperative unless it shall have been ratified as an amendment to the Constitution by the legislatures of the several States, as provided in the Constitution, within seven years from the date of the submission hereof to the States by the Congress.

Amendment 19 - Women's Suffrage.

The right of citizens of the United States to vote shall not be denied or abridged by the United States or by any State on account of sex.

Congress shall have power to enforce this article by appropriate legislation.

Amendment 20 - Presidential, Congressional Terms.

1. The terms of the President and Vice President shall end at noon on the 20th day of January, and the terms of Senators and Representatives at noon on the 3d day of

January, of the years in which such terms would have ended if this article had not been ratified; and the terms of their successors shall then begin.

2. The Congress shall assemble at least once in every year, and such meeting shall begin at noon on the 3d day of January, unless they shall by law appoint a different day.

3. If, at the time fixed for the beginning of the term of the President, the President elect shall have died, the Vice President elect shall become President. If a President shall not have been chosen before the time fixed for the beginning of his term, or if the President elect shall have failed to qualify, then the Vice President elect shall act as President until a President shall have qualified; and the Congress may by law provide for the case wherein neither a President elect nor a Vice President elect shall have qualified, declaring who shall then act as President, or the manner in which one who is to act shall be selected, and such person shall act accordingly until a President or Vice President shall have qualified.

4. The Congress may by law provide for the case of the death of any of the persons from whom the House of Representatives may choose a President whenever the right of choice shall have devolved upon them, and for the case of the death of any of the persons from whom the Senate may choose a Vice President whenever the right of choice shall have devolved upon them.

5. Sections 1 and 2 shall take effect on the 15th day of October following the ratification of this article.

6. This article shall be inoperative unless it shall have been ratified as an amendment to the Constitution by the legislatures of three-fourths of the several States within seven years from the date of its submission.

Amendment 21 - Amendment 18 Repealed.

1. The eighteenth article of amendment to the Constitution of the United States is hereby repealed.

2. The transportation or importation into any State, Territory, or possession of the United States for delivery or use therein of intoxicating liquors, in violation of the laws thereof, is hereby prohibited.

3. The article shall be inoperative unless it shall have been ratified as an amendment to the Constitution by conventions in the several States, as provided in the Constitution, within seven years from the date of the submission hereof to the States by the Congress.

Amendment 22 - Presidential Term Limits.

1. No person shall be elected to the office of the President more than twice, and no person who has held the office of President, or acted as President, for more than two years of a term to which some other person was elected President shall be elected to the office of the President more than once. But this Article shall not apply to any person holding the office of President, when this Article was proposed by the Congress, and shall not prevent any person who may be holding the office of President, or acting as President, during the term within which this Article becomes

operative from holding the office of President or acting as President during the remainder of such term.

2. This article shall be inoperative unless it shall have been ratified as an amendment to the Constitution by the legislatures of three-fourths of the several States within seven years from the date of its submission to the States by the Congress.

Amendment 23 - Presidential Vote for District of Columbia.

1. The District constituting the seat of Government of the United States shall appoint in such manner as the Congress may direct: A number of electors of President and Vice President equal to the whole number of Senators and Representatives in Congress to which the District would be entitled if it were a State, but in no event more than the least populous State; they shall be in addition to those appointed by the States, but they shall be considered, for the purposes of the election of President and Vice President, to be electors appointed by a State; and they shall meet in the District and perform such duties as provided by the twelfth article of amendment.

2. The Congress shall have power to enforce this article by appropriate legislation.

Amendment 24 - Poll Tax Barred.

1. The right of citizens of the United States to vote in any primary or other election for President or Vice President, for electors for President or Vice President, or for

Senator or Representative in Congress, shall not be denied or abridged by the United States or any State by reason of failure to pay any poll tax or other tax.

2. The Congress shall have power to enforce this article by appropriate legislation.

Amendment 25 - Presidential Disability and Succession.

1. In case of the removal of the President from office or of his death or resignation, the Vice President shall become President.

2. Whenever there is a vacancy in the office of the Vice President, the President shall nominate a Vice President who shall take office upon confirmation by a majority vote of both Houses of Congress.

3. Whenever the President transmits to the President pro tempore of the Senate and the Speaker of the House of Representatives his written declaration that he is unable to discharge the powers and duties of his office, and until he transmits to them a written declaration to the contrary, such powers and duties shall be discharged by the Vice President as Acting President.

4. Whenever the Vice President and a majority of either the principal officers of the executive departments or of such other body as Congress may by law provide, transmit to the President pro tempore of the Senate and the Speaker of the House of Representatives their written declaration that the President is unable to discharge the powers and duties of his office, the Vice President shall immediately assume the powers and duties of the office as Acting President.

Thereafter, when the President transmits to the President pro tempore of the Senate and the Speaker of the House of Representatives his written declaration that no inability exists, he shall resume the powers and duties of his office unless the Vice President and a majority of either the principal officers of the executive department or of such other body as Congress may by law provide, transmit within four days to the President pro tempore of the Senate and the Speaker of the House of Representatives their written declaration that the President is unable to discharge the powers and duties of his office. Thereupon Congress shall decide the issue, assembling within forty eight hours for that purpose if not in session. If the Congress, within twenty one days after receipt of the latter written declaration, or, if Congress is not in session, within twenty one days after Congress is required to assemble, determines by two thirds vote of both Houses that the President is unable to discharge the powers and duties of his office, the Vice President shall continue to discharge the same as Acting President; otherwise, the President shall resume the powers and duties of his office.

Amendment 26 - Voting Age Set to 18 Years.

1. The right of citizens of the United States, who are eighteen years of age or older, to vote shall not be denied or abridged by the United States or by any State on account of age.

2. The Congress shall have power to enforce this article by appropriate legislation.

Amendment 27 - Limiting Changes to Congressional Pay.

No law, varying the compensation for the services of the Senators and Representatives, shall take effect, until an election of Representatives shall have intervened.

Thanks are due to the countless individuals who heard me carry on about writing this book for the past several years. Often times it seemed that it would never see the light of day, but they each encouraged and supported me in their own way. The following is by no means exhaustive of those who deserve my gratitude.

First, to my sister Erica: your passion for the socio-economic forces driving our nation's history often helped to replenish my own energies to continue writing, editing, and revising.

To Peter Hanna: without you this project would never have begun.

To Jana Wilcox: thanks are not enough for everything you have done as a friend. Your continued support of and interest in this project helped to reinvigorate me each time we spoke.

To Richard Hayden: one could not ask for a better and more intellectually stimulating friend. Thank you for the motivation and confidence you instilled in me, especially in the final stages of this work.

To Shani: You are the love of my life. Your confidence in me encouraged the ultimate production of this work.

Selected Bibliography

The following list is far from exhaustive of the resources used in the research for this book, but forms the bulk of the reference materials used:

Aldrich, John H. (1997), *Why Parties Matter: The Origin and Transformation of Political Parties in America*, Chicago, University of Chicago Press

Bibby, John F. and L. Sandy Maisel (2003), *Two Parties – or More?: The American Party System* (2nd Ed.), Boulder, Westview Press

Boller, Jr., Paul F. (2004), *Presidential Campaigns: From George Washington to George W. Bush*, Oxford, Oxford University Press

Brands, H.W. (2000), *The First American: The Life and Times of Benjamin Franklin*, New York, Anchor Books

Brookhiser, Richard (1999), *Alexander Hamilton, American*, New York, Simon & Schuster

Chace, James (2004), *1912*, New York, Simon & Schuster

Davis, Kenneth C. (2004), *Don't Know Much About History: Everything You Need to Know About American History but Never Learned*, HarperCollins Perennial

De Tocqueville, Alexis, *Democracy in America*, Trans. George Lawrence, HarperCollins Perennial

Ellis, Joseph J. (2000), *Founding Brothers: The Revolutionary Generation*, New York, Vintage Books

Gillespie, J. David (1993), *Politics at the Periphery: Third Parties in Two-Party America*, Columbia, University of South Carolina Press

Hesseltine, William B. (1957), *The Rise and Fall of Third Parties: From Anti-Masonry to Wallace*, Washington, D.C., Public Affairs Press

Johnson, Paul (1999), *A History of The American People*, HarperCollins Perennial

Madison, James, Alexander Hamilton and John Jay (1788), *The Federalist Papers*, Penguin Classics

Reichley, A. James (1992), *The Life of the Parties: A History of American Political Parties*, New York, The Free Press

Remini, Robert V. (1988), *The Life of Andrew Jackson*, New York, HarperCollins Perennial

Remini, , Robert V. (2009), *A Short History of the United States*, HarperCollins Perennial

White, John Kenneth and Daniel M. Shea (2000), *New Party Politics: From Jefferson and Hamilton to the Information Age*, Boston/New York, Bedford/St. Martin's

Index

233

238

www.ingramcontent.com/pod-product-compliance
Lightning Source LLC
Chambersburg PA
CBHW062214270326
41930CB00009B/1738